Cicero's *Philippics* and Their

Demosthenic Model

Cecil W. Wooten

Cicero's *Philippics* and Their

Demosthenic Model

The Rhetoric of Crisis

The University of North Carolina Press

Chapel Hill and London

© 1983 The University of North Carolina Press

All rights reserved

Manufactured in the United States of America

Library of Congress Cataloging in Publication Data

Wooten, Cecil W., 1945–
    Cicero's Philippics and their Demosthenic model.

    Includes index.
    1. Cicero, Marcus Tullius. Philippicae. 2. Demosthenes—
Influence—Cicero. I. Title.
PA6280.W66 1983   875'.01   82-24857
ISBN 0-8078-1558-6

For

H. BENNETT CARR

Contents

Preface

Cicero's *Philippics* are his most mature speeches. They were delivered after more than forty years of busy, often intense activity as a courtroom advocate and as a practicing politician. During the ten years preceding the crisis that evoked them, he had been engaged in considerable speculation about oratorical technique and the nature of oratory itself. And they were delivered during one of the supreme crises of Roman history, when, after almost a century of internal discord, the direction that the Roman government would take for the next five hundred years was finally determined. Nevertheless, the *Philippics* have received very little critical attention as works of oratory. Most of the scholarship that has been done on them is historical in nature and does not deal with these speeches as rhetorical responses to distinct political situations. The purpose of this essay is to correct that lack. My goal is a fairly modest one: to deal with the various aspects of these speeches that make them effective oratory and that distinguish them from Cicero's earlier orations and to explain why they are different.

Because of their length and the complicated political situation in which they were delivered, Cicero's *Philippics* are difficult to approach; and I think that this is one reason why there has been so little interest in them as works of oratory. It has often seemed to me, however, that the best way to approach these speeches would be to compare them with those of Demosthenes against Philip of Macedon, by which Cicero was surely influenced; and this is the approach that I have taken. Cicero's political situation in 43 B.C. was generally similar to that in which Demosthenes found himself in the middle of the fourth century, and he had been reading Demosthenes extensively during the two or three years that preceded his conflict with Antony.

This work is not intended to be exhaustive. Much of it is speculative, and I have purposely neglected the historical problems that are involved. Moreover, I have generally avoided much of the apparatus of classical scholarship and most technical terminology because I have envisioned a wider audience than that to which scholarly works in classics are often addressed: students, scholars, and those engaged in other fields, such as speech communication, in addition to professional classicists. I have, however, assumed a knowledge of Latin. Much of the essay, especially chapter 6, consists of detailed stylistic analyses of sections of the *Philippics*; and to appreciate these parts of the work a knowledge of Latin is indispensable. On the other hand, I have not assumed a knowledge of Greek. The chapter on Demosthenes' style is sufficiently general to be understood by a Greekless reader and serves merely as a framework for parts of the rest of the work. There is also considerable scholarship, much of it very good, on Demosthenes' oratory. I feel sure, therefore, that those who will be attracted to this essay are primarily interested in Cicero and consequently will probably have some knowledge of Latin.

Certain portions of this book have been previously published in other forms. Much of chapter 3 originally appeared in an article entitled "Cicero's Reactions to Demosthenes: A Clarification," *Classical Journal* 73 (1977): 37–43. The section in chapter 4 on the *Fifth Philippic* appeared in "Démosthène, le mode satirique, et la *Cinquième Philippique* de Cicéron," *Les Etudes Classiques* 50 (1982): 193–200.

There are many acknowledgments that I would like to make, but there is space for only a few. I would like to thank the American Council of Learned Societies, the National Endowment for the Humanities, and the National Humanities Center for providing grants, funds, and facilities that made the writing of this work possible. I would also like to express my gratitude especially to Professor George Kennedy, without whose advice and support this essay in its present form could never have been written and whose generosity and encouragement have been invaluable to me throughout my career. Moreover, I would like to thank Professor T. R. S. Broughton, who read the manuscript and saved me from many potentially embarrassing errors, and the readers and staff of the University of North Carolina Press, especially Pam Morrison.

And I would like to acknowledge a debt of gratitude of a more general sort. Few people are lucky enough to experience the sort of friendship that Cicero so eloquently describes in the *de Amicitia*. I have been among the fortunate. Over the past twenty years, Bennett Carr's companionship, advice, and support have enriched my life more than mere words could ever express; and it is to him, therefore, that I gratefully dedicate this book.

C. W. W.
Fire Island Pines
July 1981

Cicero's *Philippics* and Their

Demosthenic Model

Chapter 1

Introduction: The Rhetoric of Crisis

Demosthenes and Cicero lived at the great turning points of Greek and Roman civilization and were major participants in the drama that would lead eventually to the establishment of the Hellenistic monarchies and the Augustan principate.[1] Their deaths mark the end of the independent city-state as the major form of government in Greece and of republican government at Rome. Both resisted these changes and devoted their rhetorical talents, which were considerable, to a vigorous defense of the status quo. It is their oratory, forged in the midst of upheaval and crisis, that is the subject of this book. Before turning to that, however, some historical background and some analysis of their character seems in order.

Early in his career, Demosthenes supported the conservative political party of Eubulus, who was in favor of abandoning Athens' maritime confederacy and turning the city into a peaceful maritime republic with a sound economic policy, and opposed Aristophon, the leader of the interventionist, imperialistic elements in the state. In his first purely political speech, we see this adherence to the conservative policies of Eubulus very clearly. Relations between Persia and Athens had been strained since 359 B.C., when Artaxerxes III came to the throne of Persia, because Athenian mercenaries had participated in revolts against the king. There were rumors that Artaxerxes was preparing for war with Athens, and the adherents of Aristophon felt that Athens should take the initiative and declare war on Persia. At an assembly held to debate this situation in 354, Demosthenes, then thirty, delivered his first public oration, *On the Symmories*. In this speech he proposed a reorganization of the naval boards, which were responsible for outfitting the fleet, in an attempt to spread the tax burden over a larger number of citizens and to lower the tax rate on the rich, who were members of the peace party of Eubulus. By his exalted demands and his descriptions of the sacrifices that a Persian war would require, Demosthenes was perhaps instrumental in avoiding a war with Persia. His proposal for the reorganization of the naval boards, however, was not put into effect until 340.

In the speech *For the Megalopolitans*, delivered in 353, Demosthenes first strikes out on his own and breaks away from the policies of Eubulus. Megalopolis had always been supported by Thebes against Sparta; however, when the Thebans became involved in the Sacred War in 355, the Megalopolitans began to fear that Sparta would renew her aggressions and appealed to Athens for an alliance. Eubulus had espoused a policy of nonintervention; but Demosthenes, arguing on the basis of the balance of power in Greek politics, supported the Megalopolitan request and tried to persuade the Athenians to build up a base of power by supporting smaller states against both Sparta and Thebes. Athens turned down the Megalopolitan request; and Megalopolis applied for help to Philip of Macedon, thus giving him the opportunity to interfere in Greek affairs for the first time.

Why Demosthenes broke with Eubulus is uncertain. It is clear that he was well acquainted with Thucydides, and the portrait presented there of the power and prestige of Athens during the fifth century may have inspired his desire for Athens to regain its former position in Greek politics. It is also obvious that Demosthenes was ambitious, and it may very well be that he was simply looking for a cause with which he might gain a political base of support and advance his own career by appealing to the former adherents of the interventionist policy of Aristophon. In any case, after 353 he was the leader of a certain faction in Athenian politics and was to remain the leader of that faction until the disastrous result of its policy at the battle of Chaeronea in 338.

The speech *For the Rhodians* is also an appeal to the people of Athens to broaden their base of power by accepting alliances with states seeking aid against greater powers. In this speech Demosthenes supports an appeal by the democratic party on Rhodes to aid them in freeing the island from the influence of Artemisia of Caria, whose husband Mausolus had brought the island under his hegemony after its revolt from the Athenian confederacy in 357 and had established an oligarchy in the island with a Carian garrison to insure its power. Demosthenes argues that Athenian help for the Rhodian democrats would be a signal for democratic parties in all the islands to rise up against oligarchies and thus could be the beginning of a renewed Athenian confederacy. Demosthenes also glances in this speech at Philip of Macedon, the problem in the north. Demosthenes feared that Philip would come to the aid of states rejected by Athens, as he had done in the case of the Megalopolitans, and thus extend his influence in Greece. If this speech was delivered soon before the *First Philippic*, it is here that Demosthenes begins to realize that Philip would become the most serious problem for Athenian foreign policy. It is in the *First Philippic*, however, probably delivered in the spring of 351, that Demosthenes deals directly with the relationship between Athens and Philip. The speech is a call to action, an appeal to the Athenians to prepare for the conflict with Philip, which Demosthenes portrays as being inevitable. It is also quite possible that Demosthenes' own intransigent attitude toward Philip was most responsible for the final conflict that would eventually come.

In 349 Athens was offered a golden opportunity. Olynthus, the most powerful Greek city in the north, appealed to Athens to make an alliance with her against Philip. Demosthenes was overjoyed and in the three *Olynthiacs* urged the Athenians to accept the alliance. Athens followed his advice; however, the Athenians, probably due to a lack of funds, sent out only small and ineffectual contingents to aid Olynthus. Demosthenes realized the absolute necessity for more war funds; and in the *Third Olynthiac* he broke completely with Eubulus, who had made his reputation as treasurer of the Theoric Fund, by proposing that the laws prohibiting the use of this fund for military purposes be repealed. This was not done, and in 348 Olynthus and all the towns of the Olynthian League fell to Philip.

Demosthenes realized that Athens was too weak to go to war with Philip; and, when efforts to unify all of Greece against Macedonia failed, Demosthenes supported a proposal by Philocrates that Athens should send ambassadors to Philip to negotiate a peace. Demosthenes was one of these ambassadors, as was Aeschines, who was to become his most implacable political rival. The ambassadors hastened to Pella and pleaded Athens' case before Philip. Demosthenes spoke last and, according to Aeschines, broke down at the beginning of his speech. In April of 346, the terms of the peace were debated at Athens and agreed to. The same ten ambassadors were sent to Pella to receive Philip's oaths to abide by the peace. When they arrived, Philip was in Thrace; and the ambassadors waited for him at Pella almost a month. This meant, of course, that whatever territory Philip subdued during this period remained in his control since the peace was based on the status quo.

Philip stipulated in the peace agreement that Phocis and Halus, both Athenian allies, were to be excluded from the treaty; and before the ambassadors could reach Athens, Philip had marched his army to Thermopylae with the obvious intent of settling the Sacred War, which had been raging in central Greece between Thebes and Phocis since 353. Thebes had applied to Philip for aid in 347.

Soon after Philip took charge of the war, Phocis surrendered. The towns of Phocis were split up, a huge fine was imposed on the Phocians, and Philip was awarded their position on the Amphictyonic Council. The swiftness with which Philip had moved against Phocis alarmed the Athenians, and they began to make preparations for war in case Philip should invade Attica. He sent assurances, however, that he had no hostile intentions toward Athens.

The years 346 to 343 were years of nominal peace between Athens and Philip. In 344 Sparta began to threaten some of the smaller states of the Peloponnesus, which applied to Philip for help. Demosthenes feared Philip's influence in the Peloponnesus and went to these cities to urge them to appeal to Athens, not Philip, which was quite in keeping with his earlier policy, seen in the speech *For the Megalopolitans*, of gaining the support of smaller states against larger ones. Philip protested these embassies to the Peloponnesus; and during a debate concerning his protests, Demosthenes delivered the *Second Philippic*, in which he argued that Philip was trying to isolate Athens from the other Greek states.

There was evidently a revival of anti-Macedonian feeling in Athens at this time, fomented mainly by Demosthenes and his political faction. The Athenians began to discuss the possibility of amending the peace they had made in 346 to read that Philip and Athens would control "what was their own" rather than "what they possessed" at the time of the treaty. These terms obviously were rejected by Philip, who, nevertheless, probably genuinely desired peace with Athens. Demosthenes and his political allies, however, were determined to provoke a conflict.

To insure her control of the grain routes, Athens had sent large numbers of colonists to settle in the Thracian Chersonesus. These settlers had come into conflict with the city of Cardia, which was allied with Philip. The Athenians sent out a military force, led by Diopeithes, to support the Athenian colonists; and Philip sent a garrison to Cardia. To maintain his army, Diopeithes attacked shipping in the north Aegean and even made raids on parts of Thrace that Philip had incorporated into his kingdom. In 341 Philip sent a strong letter of protest to Athens; it was on this occasion that Demosthenes delivered the *Third Philippic*, in which he depicts Philip as a threat not only to Athens but to all of Greece. The speech is the culmination of Demosthenes' efforts to polarize the conflict with Philip, to depict it as a desperate struggle for survival of the Greek way of life, and to force a showdown.

In accordance with the Panhellenic ideas expressed in this speech, Demosthenes began soon after its delivery to attempt to organize a Panhellenic alliance against Philip. He made many new alliances and renewed some previous ones, including an alliance with the city of Byzantium, which lay on the grain route and which Demosthenes feared Philip would attack to gain control of Athens' grain supply. In 340 Philip did attack Byzantium and seized 230 ships waiting there to be escorted to Athens; Athens declared war. Because of Athenian and Persian reinforcements, Philip had to withdraw from his siege of the city in 339 and then went north to make war on the Scythians. During this period Demosthenes began to prepare Athens for war. He put into effect the reform of the naval boards that he had proposed fifteen years earlier and succeeded in pushing through another of his earlier proposals, the use of the Theoric Fund for military purposes. Demosthenes realized that Athens had the most chance of success in a guerrilla-type war against Philip, so he tried to avoid a pitched battle. Philip realized that he would have the advantage in a battle of this sort and was awaiting an excuse to invade central Greece.

This excuse came in the early autumn of 339. In 340 Athens had regilded a thank offering that, according to the inscription, had been taken from the Persians and the Thebans. At a meeting of the Amphictyonic Council in 339, the Locrians, who had been allies of Thebes during the Sacred War, accused Athens of insulting Thebes and demanded that the city be fined. Aeschines, who happened to be the Athenian delegate, took the offensive and accused the Locrians of cultivating land sacred to Apollo. War was declared on the Locrians, but the response to the levy of troops was very slight. Demosthenes persuaded the Athenians not to take part in the war, an obvious attempt on his part to try to avoid any hostilities between Thebes and Athens since he must have realized that only the alliance of these two cities, the most powerful in central Greece, could possibly stop Philip. Thebes was unrepresented as well. Soon thereafter, because of the difficulty that the leaders of the Amphictyonic Council had in raising troops, Philip was invited to take charge of the war. He marched swiftly through Thermopylae and seized Elateia, the town that commanded the entrance into Attica and from which Philip became a threat to Thebes as well. Demosthenes proposed an alliance between Athens and Thebes in the Athenian assembly, and the motion was passed. Demosthenes himself was sent to Thebes to conduct the negotiation. He had long hoped for this alliance of Athens and Thebes, but the traditional hostility between them and the fact that most anti-Macedonian politicians in Athens were also anti-Theban had made such an alliance almost impossible. Now that Athens was being threatened at close hand, Demosthenes was able to win the support of even the most rigorous anti-Thebans.

For the next few months, the Athenians and the Thebans managed to prevent Philip from crossing the mountain passes into Boeotia. In the spring of 338, Philip allowed one of his letters to Antipater to fall into the hands of the allies; it stated that he planned to return to Macedonia in order to quell a revolt in Thrace. They thus relaxed their vigilance over the passes. Philip acted fast to seize Amphissa and to gain control of some of the passes into Boeotia. The allies withdrew to Chaeronea. In August or September of 338, the two armies met; the allies were soundly defeated by the much better trained armies of Philip. Demosthenes is said to have run away during the battle but delivered the funeral oration over those who had fallen.

In Athens preparations were made for the defense of the city; however, Philip realized how difficult it would be to defeat a maritime city without a fleet and decided to come to terms with Athens. Philip also probably wanted to keep Athens' goodwill so that he could use her fleet in the war against Persia that he was undoubtedly planning by this time. Moreover, unlike Thebes, Athens had always been hostile to Philip; and thus he did not feel that he had been betrayed by the city. He took from Athens the Chersonesus but guaranteed that Attica would not be invaded and left some of the major Aegean islands under Athenian control. The government of the city was managed, evidently quite well, by Lycurgus and Demosthenes, who devoted their attention mainly to public works in the city, for which a gold crown was proposed for Demosthenes by Ctesiphon in 336.

Athens joined the League of Corinth, which was set up by Philip to organize the Greek city-states under Macedonian control; Demosthenes, as he had surely feared, was thereby forced to assume a low profile in Greek politics. In 323, moreover, he was accused of bribery and went into exile on Aegina. However, when Athens revolted after Alexander's death, Demosthenes was recalled to the city and was active in the formation of a Greek league against Macedon. When the Greeks were defeated by Antipater in 322 at the battle of Crannon, Demosthenes, realizing that his long battle against Macedon was over, committed suicide by taking poison.

Demosthenes devoted most of his mature life to the struggle against Philip of Macedon, and he pursued his anti-Macedonian policy with a single-mindedness and tenacity that sometimes seems to have bordered on the obsessive or the hysterical. Those who disagreed with him were depicted as being corrupt and degenerate; and he portrayed himself as a man of destiny, a pure patriot, thrust into a situation that was the death struggle between democracy and tyranny, freedom and slavery. His duty was to prepare the Athenian people to undertake that struggle with the same courage and self-sacrifice that their ancestors had shown in similar crises. However, the situation was not that simple. Philip wanted alliance with Athens more than anything, so that he could use the Athenian fleet in his campaign against Persia; and it was really Demosthenes, not Philip, who polarized the struggle and provoked a conflict. He made of Philip an example, indeed, the very embodiment of that barbarism with which Greeks had always felt threatened, especially since the Persian Wars of the fifth century; and he played upon these fears with a consistency that eventually produced open conflict. One could argue that Demosthenes was inspired by a conception of national honor and grandeur that did not correspond to the political realities of the age in which he lived. One could also argue, however, that his program was simply a means of furthering his own career and of staking out a position for himself in Athenian politics by opposing the established order represented by Eubulus and his allies, and that his stance of opposition to Philip involved a certain amount of role playing, inspired by models of the fifth century, to strengthen his own political hand. What his real motivations were we will never know; but his speeches, to which I will turn later, are the best place to look in an attempt to delve into his psyche. And that is surely the key to understanding his actions.

Cicero had devoted most of his life to attaining the consulship (63 B.C.) and the influence in Roman politics that this office brought; and, being a *novus homo*, he had struggled against considerable odds. Three years after his consulship, Caesar, Crassus, and Pompey formed the First Triumvirate, a step that would ultimately lead to the dictatorships of Caesar in and after the civil war. During the period following the creation of the First Triumvirate, political activity as Cicero knew it was difficult, and after

Caesar's defeat of Pompey it was virtually impossible. Cicero's dream of exercising influence as an ex-consul in the traditional governmental apparatus of Rome was shattered. Even the courts, where he had held so much authority, were changed. All his efforts to forge for himself an important position in the Roman government must have seemed to him futile. Then Caesar was assassinated. Pompey and Crassus were already dead. The republic, the political system in which Cicero could best function and could use his oratory to the greatest advantage, seemed once again a viable alternative; and Cicero was determined not to let the opportunity slip away. As during his consulship, he was presented with the possibility of creating a third force in Roman politics, a new alliance between the extremes of right and left, between the followers of the Marian tradition, who, with Caesar, had brought in military control, and the extreme aristocrats, the *optimates* constituting the inner circle of the senate, who had always threatened, sometimes with success, to turn the state into an oligarchy. Again, Cicero, the *novus homo* who could not accept a military dictatorship that would curtail his own political activity and who had always been excluded from the inner circle of the senate, saw the chance to unite moderate members of all groups, especially the senate and the knights, into an alliance that would give him that base of support that he had lacked during most of his career; with that support he could reestablish the republican constitution in which he himself could function most effectively.

The fifteen months after the murder of Caesar in March of 44 B.C. are probably the best documented in all of Roman history. We have over two hundred letters from Cicero during this period to all the major participants in the crisis that would be the death of the Roman republic. We also have Cicero's fourteen speeches against Antony, which describe in detail all the important stages and crises in the struggle. Cicero's preoccupations are also reflected in the speculative works on which he was engaged during this period. Moreover, later imperial historians treat this episode in Roman history in great detail since it was the period when Octavian, the future emperor Augustus, first came to the fore.

Caesar had begun to let the old republican offices function more freely, although he was largely in control of the elections; and at his death Antony was consul. The Caesarians were hesitant after the death of their leader; and it seemed possible, indeed probable, that constitutional government would be restored. Cicero, in good Ciceronian fashion, and surely in imitation of the Greek model of 403 in Athens, offered a compromise, an amnesty. The assassins of Caesar would be pardoned, and Caesar's acts would be confirmed and his intentions would be honored by the senate. Slowly Antony began to regain his confidence. He began to rally support for himself among Caesar's former adherents and, most importantly, among Caesar's former troops. On 1 June he summoned the senate and tried to force through certain changes, especially in provincial commands, that would secure his own position. The senate refused; however, Antony ignored the vote of the senate and got what he wanted from the popular assembly, as the Gracchi, Caesar, and others had often done before him. Meanwhile, Octavian, Caesar's adopted heir, with the magic of Caesar's name was contesting with Antony for influence among the former Caesarians, especially the army. Throughout these months when Antony and Octavian were trying to rally the sort of support that would insure their own position, Cicero stood by helplessly, finding consolation, as he had done for much of the previous twelve years, in his books and in philosophy. He felt helpless against the military power of Antony, as he had felt helpless against the armies of Caesar. He therefore decided to go to Greece, where his son was studying, and to spend the remainder of Antony's consulship there. He would then return to Italy and attempt to restore republican government there only when Antony would be away, as governor, in Cisalpine Gaul. When Cicero was at Leucopetra in southern Italy, however, it seemed to him from the news coming from Rome that Antony was losing support and might be willing to accept the disposition of the provinces that the senate had proposed. He decided, therefore, to return to the city, which he did in August of 44. This was the transition to the final phase of his career, the most glorious and courageous of his life, a period in which he put forth all his talents and all his energy in one last desperate attempt to save the republic to which he had dedicated so much of his life and from which he had derived most of his own reputation.

Cicero's enthusiastic reception when he returned to Rome boosted his confidence. So on 3 September he attacked Antony in the senate. This, the *First Philippic*, was a moderate speech on the whole, but it showed clearly that Cicero was willing to become the leader of the opposition, to rally all loyal Romans to a defense of the republic. On 19 September Antony replied in a furious and abusive speech that attacked Cicero's whole life and career. Cicero replied with the *Second Philippic*, which effectively removed the possibility of reconciliation and polarized the conflict.

He decided to use Octavian's military strength against Antony, and then to get rid of Octavian. On 1 January the senate declared a state of martial law because Antony was attempting to eject Decimus Brutus by force from his province in northern Italy. It empowered the consuls, Hirtius and Pansa, who had been supporters of Caesar but also students of Cicero, and Octavian to protect the state against Antony. Cicero showed incredible energy in galvanizing the resources of the state against Antony, who was defeated twice in northern Italy by republican forces but at the cost of the lives of both consuls. However, after his defeats, Antony marched into Gaul, where he joined up forces with Lepidus, another ex-Caesarian. Moreover, Octavian, although he had opposed Antony in his struggle to get control of Caesar's legions, began to find it distasteful to cooperate with men such as Decimus Brutus, who had been one of his adoptive father's murderers. Also, the senate, thinking that the danger from Antony had passed once he had been defeated, began to ignore Octavian and made it clear that it did not intend to reward his veterans with land after the war was over. Therefore, to insure his position, Octavian demanded one of the consulships now vacant because the consuls Hirtius and Pansa had been killed in the war against Antony. Octavian was only nineteen at the time, and the senate refused such an unconstitutional move. Consequently, Octavian, like so many Romans of the first century before him, marched on Rome with eight legions and took the city. By applying the threat of force to the elective assembly, he was then made consul with his cousin Q. Pedius.

The real problem was that Hirtius and Pansa, because they had been supporters of Caesar but also had close links with Cicero, had acted as a buffer between Octavian and the Caesarians whom he represented and the more traditionally republican forces led by Cicero, which included the murderers of Caesar. Once the consuls were dead, however, Octavian found it difficult and dangerous to deal openly and directly with Caesar's murderers, especially since this offended many of his troops. Moreover, if Hirtius and Pansa had lived, they would probably have pursued Antony and defeated him decisively before he could join forces with Lepidus in Gaul. But their deaths in northern Italy had forestalled quick and effective action by the republican forces.

In any case, after Octavian became consul in such an unconstitutional way, Cicero once again withdrew from politics, his hopes of restoring the republic shattered, this time forever. Octavian soon realized that it was in his best interests to ally himself with Antony and Lepidus, to join forces with the other ex-Caesarians who more nearly represented the political attitudes of his own troops, especially since Brutus and Cassius were raising forces in the east that would one day be used against the Caesarians. Cicero had widespread support in Rome and Italy; but his supporters, as often, had to yield to superior military force. When Antony, Lepidus, and Octavian met near Bologna to form the Second Triumvirate and decided to draw up proscription lists to get money to reward their troops, Antony demanded that Cicero's name be put first. He was killed trying to escape to Greece to join the forces of Brutus and Cassius, and Antony had his hands and head cut off and nailed to the speaker's platform in Rome, from which Cicero had delivered many of his speeches against Antony.

One would like to eulogize Cicero, for he was in many respects the most attractive character whom antiquity produced. Once he took on the conflict with Antony, he showed tremendous energy in coordinating efforts all over the empire against him and a striking display of determination and resolution such as the often vacillating Cicero had never shown before; and his initial successes were impressive. Like Demosthenes, he portrayed himself as a man of destiny, struggling valiantly against evil and corruption for traditional ideals. However, we see in his later career, as in his earlier life, a man who really did not think deeply about the basic political, social, economic, and administrative problems of the age in which he lived and who, also like Demosthenes, often preferred to idealize the past than to face the present realistically. In many ways, what interested both Cicero and Demosthenes was not really policy or statesmanship, but politics, the opportunity to be able to exercise their oratory and to influence their fellow citizens. Many of their policies were really simply a clever politician's attempts at maintaining the status quo, for that was the system in which they themselves could function most effectively and where they could use to greatest advantage their most powerful political weapon—their oratory.

How do we account for the extreme and uncompromising stands that Demosthenes and Cicero took? or for the

tenacity and single-mindedness with which they defended those positions? In terms of motivation, effectiveness, and true conviction, they are among the most con-
troversial figures from antiquity. Some have seen in them
unselfish patriots in the purest sense of that term, coura-
geously fighting against overwhelming odds for a noble
ideal of liberty and participatory government. This ro-
mantic view, which I have at times held myself, is surely
naive. Others have looked on them as paranoid reaction-
aries with no political foresight, trying desperately to hold
back the course of history and to preserve political institutions that were outmoded and no longer viable. This
view, however, seems unfair, for it demands of them more
foresight and more understanding than most politicians
have possessed and attributes to their opponents the sort
of deep insight into the political situation that they surely
did not have. Neither of these views, moreover, establishes any psychological credibility; and without that we
can never hope to understand Demosthenes or Cicero.
Perhaps a better approach would be to suspend political
judgment and to try to understand, rather, what drove
them to act as they did; and perhaps it is only through
a penetration into their psyches that we can truly understand, and thus justify, the stands that they took.

Both Demosthenes and Cicero were of an extremely
combative nature. At the age of eighteen Demosthenes
found himself bereft of resources and forced into a struggle that lasted for years to recover his patrimony from his
guardians.[2] This experience, the first of his adult life,
surely made a deep impression on the young orator. His
eventual success against considerable odds taught him
the value of tenacity and the refusal to compromise and
must have aroused in him feelings of conceit and ambition. It also probably whetted in him an appetite for the
ostensibly noble struggle against substantial opposition.
This experience probably accounts to a great extent for
Demosthenes' almost morose seriousness and severity,
intensity, and lack of humor. At a young age he was

plunged into what was almost a struggle for existence, and this doubtlessly left an indelible mark on his psyche.

Cicero likewise struggled during his early years against the disadvantages of being a *novus homo*. His first major experience in politics, again against considerable odds, was the prosecution of Verres. This surely engendered in him respect for the value of uncompromising tenacity and a fondness, always appealing to the young, for the role of the idealist contending in a seemingly noble cause against formidable opposition. His resounding success in this trial, moreover, aroused in him tremendous personal ambition; and his attainment of every office in the *cursus honorum* at the earliest legal age only confirmed his faith in his own abilities. The precariousness of his position throughout much of his career probably caused Cicero often to overreact, and the pride he felt in having risen to the top of Roman politics, in spite of the fact that he was a *novus homo*, probably made him so sensitive to criticism. These two traits are seen nowhere better than in his reactions to the criticisms of the Neoatticists (see chapter 3).

Moreover, Demosthenes and Cicero were above all advocates. Their first successes were in the courtroom. Demosthenes was a logographer as a young man and spent much of his mature life as a litigant in court. Cicero likewise spent a considerable part of his life preparing and arguing cases in the law courts. This experience must have made them prone to look on every situation as an advocate views a case: to stake out a clear position and to defend it, with every means available, to the end. And their successes in court early in life, in spite of considerable opposition, must have given the young Demosthenes and the young Cicero tremendous self-confidence in their own abilities and their own insight. Moreover, the fact that the first major cases in which they were involved were trials in which right and wrong must have seemed so obvious doubtlessly made them prone to see other problems in this same clear-cut way.[3]

As a result of their experience as advocates, both Demosthenes and Cicero soon realized the value of oratory as the means by which they could overcome great odds and attain success; and the dedication with which they developed and honed their speaking ability is another indication of their tenacity and of their determination to be successful. The stories about Demosthenes' declamatory exercises may be apocryphal, but they are surely indications of his persistence and determination. Cicero likewise devoted much of his youth to perfecting his speaking ability and declaimed even as a mature orator.[4]

Both men also had a real nostalgia for the past, which is closely related to this tendency to interpret issues in too clear-cut a fashion and to the difficulties that they encountered in their early careers. Demosthenes was obviously well acquainted with Thucydides; and the vision of Athenian power, prestige, and heroism that he found there was to be a guiding principle throughout his life. Moreover, the struggle with his guardians plus the complicated nature of Greek politics in the fourth century must have engendered in him a real longing for the fifth century, when right and wrong, good and evil, were more apparent, when life seemed simpler, when men were more virtuous and less venal, and when Greece seemed more in control of her own destiny. Cicero was reared in a middle-class family in rural Italy that instilled in him tremendous respect for old Roman values. The complicated and rapidly deteriorating political situation that he found in Rome in the first century must have aroused in him considerable longing for the third and second centuries, when political issues were more distinct and virtue was rewarded. This nostalgia for the past is another indication of their tendency to see issues in a clear-cut, even simplistic way: former Greeks and Romans were honorable and virtuous and are constantly set in opposition to the degenerate and corrupt nature of the orator's own contemporaries.[5]

Related to this nostalgia for the past, and also to the precariousness of the situations in which they often found themselves, is the tendency to imitate role-models and to interpret events in the light of patterns seen in earlier history. Demosthenes was clearly influenced by the model of Pericles and was prone to see in the conflict with Philip a reenactment of Athens' struggle against Persia in the fifth century. Cicero also often imitated models, as will be discussed in chapter 3, and saw crises in which he found parallels from earlier events in Roman history.

The most remarkable trait in Demosthenes and Cicero, however, closely related to those tendencies that I have already discussed, is the will to survive, the most basic of human impulses. Having created for himself a major role, both as a courtroom advocate and as a politician, in the democratic city-state that he so admired, Demosthenes was determined to defend at all costs the system in which he could best function, that is, in which he could use oratory to his greatest advantage. Likewise, Cicero, having struggled most of his life to attain a position of importance in the republican government of Rome, was determined that the type of government in which he had carved out a role for himself not be undermined by autocrats who left no scope for politicians like Cicero.[6] Both men had forged with considerable exertion a major role for themselves in a certain type of political system and were therefore resolved that that system survive, for without that they themselves could not survive.[7]

However, as Buffon said, "Le style est l'homme même"; and the best way to understand the psychology of Demosthenes and Cicero is to examine the style of the speeches that they wrote. I turn, therefore, to an analysis of their oratory that will reinforce the psychological portrait already sketched.

Chapter 2

Style and Argumentation in the

Speeches of Demosthenes

Since what I will be doing in much of what follows will involve a discussion of Demosthenic influence on Cicero's *Philippics*, it seems only appropriate here to discuss in a preliminary way the most basic aspects of Demosthenes' style and argumentation. Many of the points that I make here will be refined or further illustrated in the discussion of Cicero that follows.

The hallmark of Demosthenic oratory is variety, both in style and in the modulation of tone, which is clearly related to style. Dionysius of Halicarnassus points out at the end of his essay on Demosthenes (*On Demosthenes* 43):

> Now that I have shown the qualities of Demosthenes' chosen style, the reader may examine his speeches for himself. He will observe that they are composed as I have described, now serious, austere and dignified, now pleasant and agreeable. And if he still feels in need of illustration, let him take in his hand any of the speeches, beginning at any point he wishes, and read on, analysing every sentence and seeing whether the structure is sometimes halting and broken up, sometimes coherent and compact; sometimes harshly grating on the ear, sometimes gently soothing; sometimes impelling hearers to emotion, sometimes leading gently on to moral se-

riousness; and producing different effects in the actual composition.[1]

Closely related to this variety of style is Demosthenes' keen sense of propriety, his ability to choose the form that will most vividly convey the content that he wants to express. Style in his speeches is always functional, it is never merely decoration, it always clarifies a point that he wants to make or reinforces an idea that he wants to convey to his audience.[2] In many ways, what is most striking about Demosthenes' oratory is the firm control, the ability to deal in a direct way with what is most important, which he consistently shows.[3] His oratory is flesh and bones and muscle; there is no fat. This gives to his speeches vigor, directness, and immediacy in a way that was rarely equaled in ancient oratory.

The best analysis of Demosthenes' style, and the one that brings out most clearly its variety, is that found in Hermogenes' *On Ideas*.[4] This is not the place for a detailed analysis of the system of Hermogenes, which is quite complicated; and that is not my intention here. However, a general discussion of Hermogenes' analysis, with illustrations from Demosthenes' speeches, is the best way to bring out the point that I want to make, that is, the variety of styles and the rapid change of tone that one finds in Demosthenes' speeches.

Hermogenes sees in Demosthenes' oratory seven "types" or forms of style that he calls clarity, grandeur, beauty, rapidity, character, sincerity, and force (*saphēneia, megethos, kallos, gorgotēs, ēthos, alētheia,* and *deinotēs*). What is distinctive about Demosthenes' style is the way in which all of these types, as well as delicately nuanced variations on them, are combined in his oratory. As Hermogenes says:

> All these are, as it were, woven together and interpenetrating. For such is the style of Demosthenes (Rabe 218) . . . and thus [by diversifying his style] he

has made all things fit together in his style, which
forms a unity because all the types interpenetrate in
it. And so, from all the beauties of style the one
most beautiful, the Demosthenic, has been created.
(Rabe 221)

Therefore, let us look more closely at the various types
from which, according to Hermogenes, Demosthenes'
style was created. Hermogenes divides his discussion of
clarity (Rabe 226–41) into two parts, purity (*katharotēs*)
and distinctness (*eukrineia*). Purity is concerned with the
sentence itself; distinctness is concerned with the clarity
of the speech as a whole.

A clear sentence expresses a thought that is familiar to
most people, a thought that is not esoteric. It will be expressed as a direct statement of fact, having the appearance of conversation. The structure will usually consist of
a subject, in the nominative case, and a main verb; and
the clauses will be short and complete in themselves. The
rhythm will be the loose rhythms of conversation, especially iambs.

Demosthenes is very fond of the direct style described
above, a style that depends more on statement than elaboration or embellishment, and consequently shows a preference for simple or compound sentences over periodic
sentences. Most of his sentences are fairly brief and simple in their structure, using no uncommon words, no figurative language, and clauses that are short and concise;
the elaborate sentence is used only to create a special emphasis or a special effect.[5]

Distinctness demands that the orator state clearly what
is going to be said and how it is going to be developed and
that the transitions from one thought to the next be clear
and smooth. In other words, the points that the orator
wants to make must be obvious to his audience.

Demosthenes employs many devices that make clear to
his audience the points that he wants to make. What
really holds his speeches together is the repetition of cer-

tain themes or motifs, sometimes called Demosthenic commonplaces, that appear throughout the argumentation. This repetition of certain ideas, sometimes of certain words that sum up those ideas, images, types of argument, or patterns of action makes the import of the whole speech more emphatic. This recurrence, however, is not a "heavy repetition of ideas, but a subtle process of elaboration and development bringing to light new dimensions of meaning and sensation."[6] *Philippic I*, for example, is primarily a call to action, an effort to arouse the Athenians from their inertia to take the action that Demosthenes felt had to be taken. The repetition of verbs expressing necessity or obligation throughout this speech underlines that idea. They run like a leitmotiv throughout the speech. Although, as Hermogenes points out (Rabe 238–41), Demosthenes frequently states explicitly what points he will develop at the outset of an argument, he often passes almost imperceptibly from motif to motif; there are quick but almost unnoticeable changes in thought and tone. However, since there is no effort to make more than one point at a time, it is easy for the hearer or reader to keep his bearings in the speech; and these imperceptible transitions from one thought to the next contribute to the directness of the speech by removing any appearance of hesitation. Moreover, to make his ideas more effective, he usually limits the number of points that he wants to make to a few only.[7]

Another principle of argumentation of which Demosthenes was fond is the scheme whereby the orator makes a seemingly paradoxical statement and then has an imaginary interlocutor ask him to explain. This is a clever practice, for it gains the audience's attention and stimulates the hearer to follow the rest of the speech more closely. It also gives the orator an effective means for leading into his argumentation. The begining of the argumentation of *Philippic I* is a good example. Demosthenes tells the Athenians that they must not be disheartened because "what is worst from days gone by is best as regards the future." Then the question is asked, "What then is this?" To this Demosthenes replies that the situation of Athens is bad because the Athenians have enacted none of the measures that would have amelioriated their position, which leaves hope that things will improve if they do what must be done.

The clarity of Demosthenes' style and of the organization of his speeches is indicative of the simplicity with which he viewed Athens' struggle with Philip, the advocate's tendency to see the situation in terms of black and white. It is also indicative of his tendency to stake out a firm, clear-cut, and unqualified position, to which he holds tenaciously and without compromise.

Demosthenes realized that the first requirement of any speech was that it be clear, and this accounts for the importance of *saphēneia* in his speeches. He also realized, however, that clarity can appear trite or commonplace. In his discussion of grandeur (*megethos*), Hermogenes deals with the various ways in which Demosthenes prevents the clear from seeming mundane. Hermogenes divides grandeur into six subtypes that for our purposes here can be divided into three groups: solemnity and brilliance; abundance; and asperity, vehemence, and florescence.

Solemnity (*semnotēs*) is used for universal and general statements about elevated topics such as the soul, justice, and temperance or for descriptions of glorious human deeds (Rabe 242–54). These thoughts are directly stated, without hesitation of any sort, using clauses that are short and complete and relying on the use of nouns more than verbs. To increase the dignity of the sentence, the orator uses words with broad sounds, that is, which have many long syllables and diphthongs. In other words, passages that are conversational employ the loose iambic rhythm (˘ -) into which speech most naturally falls. More oratorical and less commonplace passages should employ more artificial, more stately rhythms. In his speech *On the Crown*, for example, Demosthenes opens the sentence that describes Philip's taking of Elateia in a dactylic hexameter, the stately meter of epic poetry (*On the Crown* 143). Epic meter is appropriate for an event of this magnitude, for Elateia commanded the entrance into Attica. In general, rhythms in which there is a predominance of heavy syllables produce a slow, somber, majestic, and sententious effect since they take longer to pronounce, and such rhythms should be used in passages of great gravity and importance. Light syllables produce a more rapid effect, and rhythms in which short vowels (or light syllables) predominate should be used in more conversational passages. Blass has pointed out that Demosthenes generally avoids more than two light syllables in succession, which gives a more dignified, manly, and solemn tone to his prose.

There are many examples of solemnity in Demosthenes. The most famous is the oath by those Athenians who had fought the Persians:

> But it is not possible, it is not possible, men of Athens, that you acted wrongly when you chose to fight for the liberty and safety of all the Greeks, no, I swear it by your ancestors who fought at Marathon, by those who drew up in battle array at Plataea, by those who fought in the sea battles at Salamis and Artemisium, and by many other brave men who lie in the public sepulchers, all of whom the city buried at its own expense, thinking them worthy of the same honor, Aeschines, not just those who were successful and victorious. And justly so. For all performed the duty of brave men. Their fortune was such as heaven granted to them. (*On the Crown* 208)

One sees here the use of epanadiplosis, the repetition of a phrase to emphasize and drive home a point; the first time it is expressed in a moderate tone, then is repeated in a much more forceful tone with added vocal stress. Demosthenes especially uses this figure with negatives when he wants to insist upon the negation. One sees in this passage as well the appeal to the finest traditions of the city of Athens, which is so typical of Demosthenes.

Hermogenes recommends the use of metaphor (Rabe 248) as a device that is characteristic of solemnity, although strong metaphors are more typical of asperity (see pp. 30–31). Demosthenes uses metaphors to make an abstract idea or complicated concept clearer to his listeners and to arouse their attention. The metaphor makes his thought more vivid and puts him into closer contact with his audience. Many of his metaphors, reflecting his combative nature, are dominated by the idea of struggling, and many of them are taken from warfare. There are also metaphors from hunting, another form of combat. One sees this obsession with struggling in his metaphors taken from physical life as well, especially in metaphors concerning sickness and health. He also prefers images of the weather, a natural phenomenon against which man struggles for survival, just as, according to Demosthenes, the Athenians were struggling against Philip[8] and just as Demosthenes himself was struggling for his own political survival. Demosthenes' similes are thematically very similar to his metaphors. They also deal primarily with struggle and combat, activity and movement, sickness and health,[9] reflecting once again Demosthenes' own psychological makeup.

The most striking characteristics of Demosthenes' metaphors and similes are their simplicity and the fact that they are never added just to adorn the speech, never purely ornamental. Demosthenes' figures are always natural and appear to be spontaneous. They always have a persuasive function and are closely related to the point that the orator is making. In fact, this repetition of certain images is typical of Demosthenes' emphatic style and is intended to plant certain concepts deeply in the minds of his listeners through a recurrence of certain motifs, which often contributes significantly to holding the speech together.[10]

Brilliance (*lamprotēs*) is closely related to solemnity.

Again the speaker uses this type of style when he has confidence in what he is saying, that is, when he is saying what is generally approved by or what will please the audience (Rabe 264–69). The difference between solemnity and brilliance is related to content. The orator uses brilliance when he is describing a noble act of less universal import than those glorious deeds that would be described by solemnity, when he is discussing, for example, his own acts as opposed to those of his ancestors. The style is basically the same as the solemn except that the clauses are often rather long and use amplification:

> I did not fortify the city with stones or with bricks, nor do I pride myself especially on these works. But if you want to consider my fortifications justly, you will find weapons and cities and outposts and seaports and ships and horses and many ready to fight for them. (*On the Crown* 299)

As Hermogenes points out (Rabe 242), it is amplification or abundance (*peribolē*), the second major element of grandeur, that Demosthenes uses most often to give emphasis to a thought and to lift it above the commonplace (Rabe 277–96). Many of the techniques that make the style full are seen in the following passage:

> What Philip took and held before I became a politician and a public speaker, I will pass over. (1) For I think that none of these gains concerns me. (2) But what he was prevented from doing from the day when I turned my mind to political affairs, I will remind you of and give an account of them, premising only the following. (3) A great advantage, men of Athens, existed for Philip. (4) For among the Greeks, not some, but all alike, it happened that there was a crop of traitors and venal politicians and men hateful to the gods such as no one ever remembers having existed before. (5) Having taken these as assistants and accomplices, he made the Greeks, who

> even before had been badly disposed to one another
> and quarrelsome, even more so, deceiving some, and
> bribing others, and corrupting others in every way,
> and he split them into many factions, although one
> thing was beneficial to them all, to prevent him
> from becoming greater. (*On the Crown* 60–61)

Many elements in this passage amplify the thought. There
is antithesis and parallelism in the first sentence and the
third; however, as usual, Demosthenes avoids the strict,
obvious antitheses of the Gorgianic style. He never allows
the desire for contrast or parallels to control his thought.
He often purposely disturbs a perfect balance to make the
expression seem more natural while still retaining the
emphatic contrast achieved by the use of an antithetical
structure.[11] Antithesis for Demosthenes was a much more
flexible means of expression than it was for Gorgias or
Isocrates. He controls the style; the style does not control
him. Demosthenes' antitheses, moreover, all grow out of
the thought. He usually prefers equivalence, or antithesis
of ideas, to detailed antithesis in structure, for this shows
more sincerity and appears to be more natural and truth-
ful than strict antithesis. He uses antithesis and parallelism only when it fits his design, when it heightens, say,
the irony of a contrast, such as "from small and humble
Philip has grown great" (*Philippic III* 21).[12]

In this passage, too, is seen Demosthenes' fondness for
the figure of speech called synonymity, the repetition of
nearly synonymous words to allow the speaker to emphasize and dwell upon an idea. These synonyms give the
passage more weight and majesty and the sort of repetition that contributes to the clarity of the speech. They
force the attention of the hearer on an idea that he might
pass over otherwise and fix the idea in his mind. There is
generally no real difference between the synonyms except
that the first is often more general.[13] The synonyms, moreover, are often arranged in groups of three and become
more intense or more general as they progress (climax);

and Demosthenes quite often uses polysyndeton to allow him to linger even longer on each component that makes up the group, as he does in the fifth sentence quoted above.[14]

The goal of abundance is to make the thought clear, vivid, and emphatic; and its importance in the speeches of Demosthenes is another indication of the clarity and directness with which he viewed Athens' conflict with Philip. There is no hesitation, no doubt; the issue to him is clear-cut and obvious.

The third group comprising grandeur is composed of asperity (*trachutēs*), vehemence (*sphodrotēs*), and florescence (*akmē*). These three share a common feature: they all involve criticism or reproach.

Asperity (Rabe 254–60) is the style to be used when the orator is making an open reproach of someone or some group more important than himself. The style is often figurative, usually uses very short clauses and often simple phrases, and takes no notice of sounds that clash. Indeed, by means of this style, the orator attempts to produce a harsh effect in order to convey anger or impatience:[15]

> When, therefore, Athenians, will you do at last what must be done? What are you waiting for? Until, by Zeus, it is necessary. But now how should one consider what has happened? For I think that for free men shame because of their position is the greatest compulsion. Or, tell me, do you want to run around and ask one another, "Is there some news?" For what could be more shocking news than that a Macedonian is making war on the Athenians and managing the affairs of the Greeks? "Has Philip died?" "No, by Zeus, but he is sick." And what does it matter to you? For indeed, if he dies, swiftly you would create another Philip, if this is the way you manage your affairs. (*Philippic I* 10)

The rhetorical questions and the exclamations give the impression that Demosthenes' anger and impatience have spontaneously burst forth and are intended to provoke the same reaction from his audience. By being angry himself, he attempts to make his audience angry. Questions, direct forms of address, and parenthetical expressions such as "tell me" give an air of spontaneity and liveliness to the passage and put the orator in closer contact with his audience. The imaginary dialogue that Demosthenes uses here is intended to have the same effect on the auditor as the rhetorical question, to strike him with the foolishness of the situation as the orator presents it and to arouse his indignation. Demosthenes' own answers to the imaginary questions of the Athenian populace underline the seriousness of the situation and the naiveté of the Athenian people. The short sentences, spoken one right after the other with no connectives, also create an air of passion and rapidity of proof. The irony and sarcasm of the last sentence are intended to shame, even to anger, the people into taking some action. The whole passage is a call to action, an attempt to provoke the people by means of a passionate appeal to do what Demosthenes felt had to be done. The passage has great force. It is intended to shock and arouse. Through the use of the dramatic imaginary scene, the orator causes the reader or audience to feel what he feels. One can only imagine how forceful it must have been when delivered by an orator as consummate at delivery as Demosthenes is supposed to have been.[16]

Vehemence (Rabe 260–64) should be used for reproach or abuse directed against people who are considered inferior to the orator. The charges are made very openly, and there is no mitigation of the criticism since the audience would receive it gladly. The best examples of vehemence in Demosthenes are those passages that he directs against Aeschines in the speech *On the Crown* (cf. 121, 127, 209), but there are also examples in the speeches against Philip:

> Although he is not only not a Greek, nor related to the Greeks in any way, but not even a barbarian from a place that is respectable, but a wretched Mac-

edonian, from an area from which it was not even possible to buy a decent slave before. (*Philippic III* 31)

Florescence (Rabe 269–77) is like vehemence or asperity in that it is appropriate for criticism. However, just as the vehement style makes criticisms more openly and more harshly than asperity, florescence is used when the orator wants to make reproaches in a gentler manner; it is "expansive where the others are concise."[17] In other words, by using longer clauses, with amplification and figures of speech, such as the anaphora which one sees in the following passage, he mitigates the element of anger in the reproach and makes the criticism in a less accusatory fashion:

It would not have been safe to plead Philip's cause in Olynthus unless the people of Olynthus were being benefited by sharing the revenues from Potidaea. It would not have been safe to plead his cause in Thessaly unless the majority of the Thessalians had benefited by his driving out the tyrants and giving them back the right of sending deputies to the Amphictyonic Council. It would not have been safe in Thebes until he had given back Boeotia and destroyed the Phocians. But at Athens, although Philip not only has snatched from you Amphipolis and Cardia, but also is preparing Euboea as a seat of operations against you and is now proceeding on the way to attack Byzantium, it is safe to speak on his behalf. (*On the Chersonese* 65–66)

These three subtypes, asperity, vehemence, and florescence, inject an element of passion into the speech. They lift it above the commonplace by giving certain passages an air of the sort of spontaneity that is provoked by anger. The frequency with which Demosthenes uses such passages is another indication of the vehemence with which he waged the battle against Philip.

Just as anaphora and other figures of speech often associated with poetry can be used to mitigate passages of criticism or reproach, such figures can be used throughout the speech to give it some ornamentation, which charms and delights the audience with carefully chosen and meticulously wrought language. This aspect of the speech Hermogenes deals with under beauty (*kallos*). This style, which is usually associated with Isocrates, is relatively rare in Demosthenes, who generally avoided apparent artificiality in his style (Rabe 296–311); but there are examples. Demosthenes sometimes uses climax, for instance, the repetition of the last word of a clause at the beginning of the following clause:

> I did not speak without making proposals, nor did I make proposals without serving as an ambassador, nor did I serve as an ambassador without persuading the Thebans. (*On the Crown* 179).

This passage also uses antithesis; and all of these figures create a pleasing and charming effect, which also impresses the thought on the audience.

Hermogenes associates beauty with the oratory of Isocrates, whose hallmark is the periodic style. Something should be said, therefore, about Demosthenes' use of this style. The period is a full combination of several thoughts into one independent sentence. Its hallmark is subordination. The period is so constructed that the various ideas that make up the sentence are "rounded off" at the end into a complete thought. All the clauses in the sentence are subordinated to and directed toward the completion of a single thought that is expressed in the principal clause. The period, therefore, expresses in one sentence a whole situation, that is, an action with the attendant circumstances that produced it and the consequences that followed upon it.

The period is composed of thought elements or clauses that are called *membra*. (There is here an analogy to the human body, the source of much critical terminology in

antiquity, where the limbs make up the whole.) The
membra are composed of smaller elements, such as prepositional phrases, which are called *incisa*. The classical
period was thought of as having four *membra* or clauses,
each of approximately sixteen syllables, the normal breath
span; however, the best stylists vary the length of the
clauses to avoid monotony. Demosthenes quite often al-
ternates long and short clauses within the period, and in
his speeches one often finds long periods alternating with
shorter sentences that sum up the idea in the period.

Sometimes variety is achieved by the insertion of long
sentences between periods that use coordination rather
than subordination to unite the thoughts. He uses this coordinate construction when dealing with disparate ideas
that in themselves lack unity and organization. Demosthenes realized that it was more effective to blend his
well-constructed periods with sentences of a looser and
freer construction. Even his periods are sometimes spacious and sometimes compact, and his spacious periods
are always flowing and unartificial. He combined the
elaborate and the simple, the periodic and the unperiodic,
the strained and the relaxed.

There are three types of period.[18] There is first what
one might call the analytical period, a type of sentence
in which the principal thought is stated first in an independent clause and then all the ramifications and consequences of that thought are expressed in subordinate
clauses. The sentence opens up successively to different aspects of one single idea that is expressed in the
main clause. It often progresses from the particular to
the general and from the real to the ideal, especially in
Demosthenes:

> What language should have been used, what pro-
> posal made by an adviser of the people of Athens (for
> indeed this makes a great difference), when I was
> conscious that from all time up until the day when I
> myself ascended the speaker's platform our country

had always struggled for renown and honor and glory and that she had expended both more money and more lives in behalf of her honor and the common welfare of all than the other Greeks had spent only on their own behalf, and since I knew that Philip himself, against whom we were struggling, for the sake of empire and power had had an eye knocked out, fractured his collar bone, broken his hand and his leg, was willing to lose any part of his body fortune demanded, provided that there should be a life of honor and glory for the rest? (*On the Crown* 66–67)

This is the most direct type of period since it states the main thought at the very beginning, thus putting the audience in possession at the outset of what is most important, and then spins out the ramifications and consequences of it. Demosthenes, a basically direct and analytical man, preferred this type and it could appropriately be called the Demosthenic period.

The second type, the suspenseful period, is just the opposite of the first since the full meaning is kept suspended until the end. In this type of period, the thought grows through subordinate clauses but is not completed until it reaches the end of the period, where the principal clause is located. This type of period builds up; the former works down. Although Demosthenes really prefers the first type, he does sometimes use this sort of periodic structure:

If all the results of the peace that were promised to you have happened, and if you confess that you are filled with such cowardice and wickedness that although there were no enemy troops in your land and you were not being besieged by sea and the city was in no other danger, but you were buying grain at a low price and other conditions were no worse than now, knowing in advance and hearing assurances from these men both that your allies would be de-

stroyed and the Thebans would grow strong and that
Philip would gain control of the affairs in Thrace
and would set up in Euboea bases of attack against
you and that all things that have been done would
happen, if then you cheerfully made the peace, ac-
quit Aeschines and do not add perjury also to such
serious disgraces. (*On the False Embassy* 218–19)

After such a long and elaborate period, Demosthenes often uses a very short sentence that sums up his thought:
"For he has done you no wrong but I am mad and I was
full of folly to accuse him."

The third type is the logical period, in which the clauses
that set the stage for the principal verb of the sentence,
such as cause and attendant circumstance, come before
the main clause and those clauses that express actions or
ideas that logically follow the main idea in the sentence,
such as result, come after the main clause:

When Philip had sworn to the peace and had secured
Thrace because of these men who did not obey my
decree, he bribed them to prevent our leaving Macedonia until he had made ready the preparations for
his campaign against the Phocians, in order that, if
we should announce to you here that he was intend-
ing and making preparations to march, you might
not set out and sailing with your fleet to Thermopylae block the passage as you did before but that you
might hear us reporting these things when he was
already on this side of Thermopylae and you could
do nothing. (*On the Crown* 32)

Demosthenes uses this logical period more often than he
does the suspenseful period discussed above, especially in
relating the unified nature of a series of historical events.

The period is a vertical expression. It builds up to or
works down from a central point, which is the main clause.
The other ways of joining thoughts together are horizon-

tal expressions; they lack the unity and organization of the period. Placing thoughts side by side in simple independent sentences or joining them together by coordinate conjunctions expresses a series of ideas that are not closely united. A series of actions or thoughts that are essentially unified are best expressed by means of the periodic structure.

Beautiful language tends to distend the speech, to relax and soften its intensity. This style can be used to beguile members of the audience when the orator does not want them to examine his thoughts too closely.[19] Often, however, it is appropriate to compress the argument, to sketch out a situation or point as rapidly as possible, to give energy and vivacity to the speech, again in an attempt to convey the impatience or excitement of the orator. Hermogenes deals with this style under the heading of rapidity or *gorgotēs* (Rabe 312–20). It is characterized by very short, choppy sentences that are often composed of short questions, quick replies, and sharp antitheses, and it often involves the use of trochaic rhythms:

> But this is not possible, it is not. For why would you have summoned them at this crisis? For peace? But all enjoyed peace. For war? But you yourselves were discussing terms of peace. (*On the Crown* 24)

> "By Zeus, the men are wretched and exceedingly stupid." To be sure, but still it is necesary that they be saved. For it is beneficial to Athens. (*On the Chersonese* 16)

Demosthenes, who was a nervous and excitable man, is very fond of this style; and the frequency with which one finds it in his speeches is indicative of the intensity and impatience with which he carried on his struggle against Philip.

Hermogenes' fifth type of style, *ēthos* or character, is somewhat more difficult to comprehend than the others since it does not seem to be a style so much as a type of argument. It is a collection of several types of style, most of them similar to those that have been discussed before, whose purpose is somehow to express the orator's character in an attempt to win the goodwill of the audience. In other words, it is a collection of various approaches whose purpose is to accomplish what Aristotle had called the ethical appeal.

The first of these approaches is simplicity or *apheleia* (Rabe 322–29), a style similar to clarity but whose purpose is to convince the audience that the orator is the sort of man who can perceive and explain complex issues in a simple and comprehensible way. By this means the orator attempts to win their goodwill and their trust. A remarkable example is found in the *Third Philippic* when Demosthenes has been discussing why the affairs of Greece were in such a sorry state in the fourth century:

> What then is the cause of this? For not without reason and a just cause were either the Greeks then so disposed toward liberty or those now so ready for slavery. There was something, men of Athens, something in the attitudes of the masses that does not exist now, something that triumphed over the wealth of the Persians and that kept Greece free and that was never defeated by sea or land, but now the fact that it has been lost has ruined everything and has thrown our affairs into confusion. What then was this? Nothing recondite or subtle, but that all hated those who took bribes from men who wanted to rule or to destroy Greece, and it was very serious to be convicted of taking bribes, and they punished the bribe taker with the greatest severity and there was no appeal and no pardon. (36–37)

Here Demosthenes has explained a very complex phenomenon in a very simple way, using language that is clear and straightforward, in an attempt to convince his audience that he is the sort of man who should be believed because of his clear insight into difficult situations and his ability to explain complex matters in a direct way.

There are three other approaches that can contribute to winning the goodwill of the audience: sweetness or *glukutēs* (Rabe 330–39), subtlety or *drimutēs* (Rabe 339–45), and modesty or *epieikeia* (Rabe 345–52). Sweetness charms and delights the audience by injecting poetic elements into the speech, elements similar to those discussed under beauty but of a more poetical rather than oratorical nature, such as the phrase "made the danger pass away like a cloud" (*On the Crown* 188), so admired by Longinus (*On the Sublime* 34.4). Subtlety impresses the audience with the orator's intelligence by showing his ability to express his thoughts in a striking and clever way: "But I do not fear that Philip is alive but that in Athens the spirit that hates and punishes wrongdoers is dead" (*On the False Embassy* 289). Finally, modesty tries to convince the audience that the speaker is a naturally humble and unpretentious person, so that the audience will sympathize with him more readily. This approach is seen most clearly in the speech *On the Crown*:

> But if I address myself to what I have accomplished in politics, I will often be forced to speak about myself. I will try to do so as modestly as possible, and he who has started this controversy is the one to blame for the fact that the situation necessitates this. (4)

Here Demosthenes wins the audience's goodwill by convincing them that he will praise his own accomplishments only against his will.

The ethical appeal is extremely important in the speeches of Demosthenes, especially in his greatest speech, *On the Crown*. He can convince the audience that only he has a clear insight into the situation at hand and can explain it precisely, only he can sweep the audience away with the beauty of his language and the cleverness of his expression, and he alone can win their goodwill by convincing it that he is basically a humble and modest man who speaks out only because he must (cf. *Philippic I* 1).

Hermogenes' next type, verity or sincerity (*alētheia*), is closely related to *ēthos* (Rabe 352–68) in that its effect on the audience is to project an image of "one plain-dealing man addressing another in whose judgment he has perfect confidence."[20] Sincerity is reflected in passages such as prayers, oaths, and exclamations of surprise that appear to be spontaneous outbursts on the part of the speaker. Such passages must be introduced without connectives or transitions and without any sort of preparation so that they will appear to have burst forth from the soul of the orator without having been thought out in advance:

> And in your presence, men of Athens, I call on all the gods and goddesses who protect the land of Attica, and Pythian Apollo, who is the city's ancestral god, and I pray to them all. (*On the Crown* 141)

Anacolutha and sudden reproaches, which give the impression that the orator has suddenly been carried away by emotion or is composing his speech extemporaneously, also convey sincerity:

> Therefore, since a righteous and just verdict has been indicated to all—but it is necessary that I, although I am not a slanderer. . . . (*On the Crown* 126)

To give an impression of spontaneity, the orator will also use figures of speech such as apostrophe, diaporesis, correctio, unfinished enumerations, and parentheses that seem to occur to him on the spot:

> Why you, you—calling you what would anyone address you aptly—was there any occasion when you were present. . . . (*On the Crown* 22)

And to convey his emotion he will use short clauses and broken rhythms that Hermogenes has already associated with vehemence. Finally, there is a minor subdivision of sincerity, weightiness or *barutēs* (Rabe 364–68), that basically involves the use of irony, which also reflects a candid relationship between the orator and his audience.

There are many examples of the sincere style in Demosthenes. Indeed, the first impression that the reader gets from his speeches is one of extreme earnestness. Prayers and oaths especially, such as the famous oath by those who died at Marathon, appear at points in the speech when the orator seems carried away by emotion; and there are many passages in which he seems to lose track of his train of thought or to be incapable of expressing what he feels because of the intensity of emotion that he experiences. These passages bring out once again the fervor and vehemence with which he combated Philip.

Hermogenes' seventh type, gravity, force, or *deinotēs* (Rabe 368–80), is simply the correct use of all the previously discussed types of style at the proper time and in the proper place. As I indicated earlier in this essay, he considers this the hallmark of Demosthenic oratory and the real secret of his power. It is responsiblc for the extreme modulation of tone in Demosthenes' speeches. As Dionysius of Halicarnassus says: "Whenever I pick up any of the speeches of Demosthenes, I am filled with emotion and I am driven in this direction and that, feeling one emotion after another, disbelief, anguish, fear, scorn, hatred, pity, goodwill, anger, envy, all the emotions that can move the mind of man" (*On Demosthenes* 22). Hermogenes points out, however (Rabe 381, 383–84), in spite of his frequent declaration that all the types are found comingled in the style of Demosthenes, that clarity, character, sincerity, and rapidity are most characteristic of Demosthenes' style.

The system of Hermogenes was devised to describe the

style of Demosthenes, and it brings out very well the variety and flexibility of his oratory:

> The aim of Clarity is that the audience should understand what is said, whereas Grandeur is designed to impress them with what is said. Beauty is designed to give pleasure, Speed to avoid boredom, Ethos helps to win over the audience by allying them with the speaker's customs and character, and Verity persuades them he is speaking the truth. Finally Gravity . . . stirs up the audience, and they are carried away by the completeness of the performance, not only to accept what they have heard, but to act upon it.[21]

This stylistic versatility is one of the most characteristic features of Demosthenes' eloquence. His use of argumentation was also unique in many ways, and something should now be said about that.

In the fifth century, orators tended to focus on a single argument, especially the argument from expediency.[22] In the fourth century, however, Isocrates, probably under the influence of Plato, tried to make oratory appear more moral. He popularized the practice of combining several arguments, honor, justice, and expediency, in a single speech. The early speeches of Demosthenes follow this practice; thus, *On the Symmories* and *On the Rhodians* employ appeals to expediency, honor, and justice. In the *Philippics*, Demosthenes returns to the fifth-century practice, seen most clearly in the speeches in Thucydides, of focusing on a single argument, especially the argument from expediency. To regain the vigor and directness of using a single argument and maintain the ethical and moral qualities of a synthesis of arguments, Demosthenes identified expediency, Athens' self-interest, with the preservation of Athenian national tradition. He appeals to Athenian patriotism in an effort to persuade the populace that the course of action that he proposes is the only course worthy of them. He is constantly holding up to the Athenians events in their earlier history, such as the Persian Wars, of which they would be extremely proud, in an attempt to rouse them to action through shame at the contrast between how they were acting and how their ancestors had acted.[23]

In the arrangement of his speeches, both deliberative and judicial, Demosthenes abandoned the traditional rhetorical schema of proemium, narration, confirmation, refutation, and epilogue that was most typical of judicial speeches, except that his proemia and epilogues are usually distinct. The latter are quiet in tone, often containing prayers or wishes for the future. The main function of his epilogues is generally to recapitulate his major points and repeat his concrete proposals. Although some rhetoricians recommended an emotional close to the speech, Demosthenes preferred a calm, quiet ending, as did most Attic orators, which leaves the impression that his advice has been reasonable and based on facts.

What comes between is ordered in various ways and usually combines narration, confirmation, and refutation, a versatile arrangement that Demosthenes probably took from Isaeus. Demosthenes was quite clever at using narration as a means of argumentation and at keeping the attention of his audience by combining passages of narrative, confirmation, and refutation. In some ways, a formal narration is not necessary in a deliberative speech. Demosthenes, however, like Cicero, realized how effective narration could be, not only in proving a point but also in evoking a desired emotional reaction, or in drawing historical parallels or contrasts; both were aware that in giving advice on a particular problem it was necessary to describe clearly the situation that produced the problem.[24]

In arranging the argumentation of his speeches, Demosthenes quite often places his specific proposal in the very center, flanked on either side by a general discussion of the situation that has made the proposal necessary. In the third section of the speech, which follows the nucleus of the argumentation, he often returns to points that were made in the general discussion preceding the specific proposal. What he wants to do is to prepare his audience to receive his proposal by showing them that the general situation makes such action necessary and then, having made the proposal, to return to a discussion of the general situation to show how the specific proposal can alleviate the difficulty.

In *Olynthiac I*, the section preceding the concrete proposal contains several Demosthenic commonplaces: all democracies are opposed to a monarchial form of government (2–7); Athens must seize the opportunity that the gods, who have always been on the side of the city, have offered to her in making possible an alliance with Olynthus (8); Philip has grown great because Athens has neglected her interests (9–15); Demosthenes will propose what he thinks is best for the state, whether he thinks that it will be popular or not, since this is really what is wrong in the state, that orators have spoken only to please for thirty years (16). Then there is the specific proposal that Athens send out two expeditionary forces and levy a war tax. In the third section, he returns to the general motifs of the first: just as the situation is most opportune for Athens, it is most difficult for Philip (21–24); Athens must act quickly to keep the war from Attica herself (25–27). *Olynthiac II* and *Philippic I* show this same sort of symmetry, in which general discussion of the situation is framed around a specific proposal (the *cardo* or hinge of the speech).

Even the earlier political speeches show a preference for this sort of arrangement. In the speech *For the Megalopolitans*, Demosthenes arranges his arguments almost in a circle around his main idea that Athens should keep both Sparta and Thebes weak rather than allying with either one (23). Likewise, in the speech *On the Symmories*, Demosthenes' specific proposal for reorganizing the naval boards stands in the middle of the argumentation (14 – 28), flanked on either side by more general discussions of Athens' relationship with the Persian king. Even the speech *Against Leptines*, which is loosely composed and in which the arguments seem to be lined up one right after the other, all introduced by the same transitional particle, shows this sort of symmetry in a sense. The considerations at the beginning (5 – 57) and end (88 – 162) of the argumentation are of a more general nature than those in the center, where Demosthenes discusses the honors granted to Chabrias and Ctesippus, in whose favor he was speaking. *On the Crown* shows the same sort of arrangement. Here Demosthenes deals with the technical charges involved only after he has focused the jury's attention on the larger issues, identified himself with Athens, and thus obtained the jury's goodwill.

These ideas will be discussed more fully when we look at the Demosthenic influence on Cicero's *Philippics*. Before doing that, however, it is necessary to determine exactly what Cicero's attitude towards Demosthenes was and how and why it changed in the course of his career. That will be the goal of the next chapter.

Chapter 3

Cicero and Demosthenes:

Nec Converti ut Interpres, Sed ut Orator

Roman education, both moral and literary, was based on the imitation of examples. This practice, stemming from a cyclical view of history and a static view of human nature, encouraged literary imitation and historical role playing. In his youth Cicero had imitated the style of L. Crassus and Hortensius:[1] his political views owed much to the influence of those of L. Crassus and M. Aemilius Scaurus, whose careers were an inspiration to him.[2] Coming from a family that did not have a political tradition of its own, he turned for inspiration to the careers of his mentors. It is not surprising, therefore, to find that in his later life, as in the earlier period, he was greatly influenced by models for imitation, both in style and political activity.

The influence of Demosthenes on Cicero has never been accurately assessed, and this whole question has been clouded by vague and unfounded assumptions. I will attempt to show in this chapter that Cicero started his career with little interest in or admiration for Demosthenes, then, because of his controversy with the Neoatticists, began to imitate his style and use of argumentation, and ended his career by trying to imitate the political role that Demosthenes had taken.

Demosthenes is not mentioned even once in Cicero's

treatise *On Invention*, and, more significantly, his earlier speeches show very little influence of the more striking features of Demosthenes' oratory.[3] Cicero makes no real effort in his earlier speeches to imitate any of the practices discussed in the preceding chapter. The *Verrines* are filled with stylistic excesses and are developed in a linear way. Likewise, in the speech *On the Manilian Law*, Cicero's earliest deliberative oration (although the section on Pompey could be considered panegyric), the scheme is linear and the middle style, characterized by balance, parallelism, synonymity, and figures of speech, all the elements that add "charm" to language (cf. *Orator* 91–97), is used throughout, even in the narrative sections (cf. 4–5) and the more emotional sections (cf. 29–35); here Cicero is clearly trying to include all the arguments possible (cf. 7–19), which he strings together in a linear fashion. The *Catilinarian Orations* show a looser organization than the speech *On the Manilian Law*, some effort to concentrate on crucial arguments, and more of an attempt to suit style to content (cf. *Against Catiline* 3.10–13). The organization is still relatively linear, however; and the florid, strictly antithetical style, often associated with Cicero, is still predominant (cf. *Against Catiline* 3.1–2).[4] These speeches show Cicero as a more mature orator; they do not, however, show any real influence of Demosthenes.[5]

Nevertheless, with the *Catilinarians* Cicero had gained a great political victory; and he must have begun to think of himself in reference to the great politicians of the past. For example, he writes in 60 to Atticus (*Letters to Atticus* 2.1.3) that Demosthenes had shown himself a serious politician in the *Philippics* and that he himself would like to leave behind some similar examples of his statesmanship that might be called "consular" speeches. This is Cicero's first reference to Demosthenes and is not an indication that he had any great admiration for him or saw himself as being similar to him except in very general terms, namely, that they were both statesmen. Indeed, Cicero had achieved a temporary success; Demosthenes had failed. Moreover, the reference to Demosthenes is really evoked by the fact that Atticus had lived in Greece: Cicero refers to him as *tuus Demosthenes*.[6]

In the treatise *On Oratory*, written in 55, Demosthenes is not singled out as the greatest Greek orator or politician, and Cicero's praise of him is not effusive.[7] Demosthenes' "force" or "power" (*vis*) is referred to three times (1.89, 260; 3.28), and in the third instance it is praised no more warmly than Lysias' precision or Isocrates' grace of style. He is spoken of twice as a *perfectus orator*, the first time coupled with Hypereides (1.58) and the second with Pericles (3.71). His wisdom is referred to twice (1.58, 89), although in the first instance the possibility is raised that he may have known less about politics than Lycurgus or Solon.

However, sometime between Cicero's publication of *On Oratory* in 55 and the publication of the *Brutus* and the *Orator* in 46, the Neoatticism movement appeared in Rome. One of the problems that the Neoatticists raised was the choice of models, whose importance has been pointed out above. They argued that the plain style of Lysias, characterized by the language of everyday life, avoidance of rhythm and elaborate periods, and the moderate use of figures of thought, was the true Attic style (*Orator* 24–32, 76). This criticism was aimed at Cicero, and he obviously had to reply. Isocrates, who had probably influenced him more than any other Greek orator,[8] was clearly unacceptable as a model because he embodied most of the faults to which the Neoatticists objected. The only choice left, really, was Demosthenes because Hypereides was also admired by the Neoatticists. Although in a sense the choice was forced on Cicero, in his defense of Demosthenes as an embodiment of true Attic style, he discovered what is really the hallmark of his oratory, its variety. For the first time, the essential feature of his style was brought to light, not only in Cicero's life but in Demosthenic criticism. Cicero argued in the *Orator* (76–101) that the plain style was not the only Attic style and that the truly great orator was the one who could employ all three styles, the plain, the middle, and the grand, as the occasion and the subject matter demanded, thus forcing back on Demosthenes, anachronistically, the categories of style that had been defined after his death.[9] The plain style should be used to instruct, the middle to please, and the grand to arouse the emotions. Demosthenes could speak calmly; Lysias, however, could not speak with passion.

Cicero's praise of Demosthenes in the rhetorical works that he wrote as an answer to the Neoatticists in 46 is effusive.[10] Demosthenes is spoken of again and again as being the best Greek orator by far.[11] Moreover, in the *Orator*, Cicero first compares himself to Demosthenes as an orator: "Vides profecto illum multa perficere, nos multa conari, illum posse, nos velle quocumque modo causa postulet dicere" (105). It is quite clear that Cicero had also come to recognize other aspects of Demosthenes' oratory, apart from his adroit use of style, that had made him the greatest Greek orator: the clever arrangement of the material in his speeches (*Orator* 26, 110), his excellent use of figures of thought (*Orator* 136; *Brutus* 141), his alternation of long periods with shorter sentences that often sum up the thought in the period (*Orator* 226), and his good use of prose rhythm (*Orator* 234). Cicero had begun to wonder how well he himself measured up to Demosthenes as an orator in respect to all of these practices.[12]

Now, not long after the publication of the *Brutus* and the *Orator*, that is, after the death of Caesar in 44, Cicero found himself for the first time in his life in a political situation that was not unlike Demosthenes' position as regards Philip. In his conflict with Antony, Cicero must have realized, as Demosthenes did, that he was involved in a struggle for survival, not only of the republican constitution but, more importantly, of the only type of government in which he could function effectively. In other words, his own survival as an orator and a politician begins to be identified with the survival of the republican constitution in terms of which he had come to define himself. Cicero soon realized, therefore, that the speeches of Demosthenes were for him more than stylistic models; they were models of the type of deliberative oratory, motivated by the impulse for survival, in which he himself would be engaged.[13]

A few references from Cicero's letters support this conclusion. In May of 44, Cicero sent Atticus a letter (*Letters to Atticus* 15.1a) in which he states that he had been asked to criticize a speech delivered by Brutus on the Capitol after the assassination of Caesar. Although he admires the speech, he argues that he would have spoken *ardentius*. He asks Atticus to read Brutus's speech and, if he is tempted to make "attic" criticisms, to remember how Attic were the *fulmina* of Demosthenes. Cicero is clearly implying that the occasion had demanded the "thunderbolts" of Demosthenes; and it is not unlikely, I think, that even in May Cicero was beginning to realize that the struggle would be one for self-preservation and that an orator like Demosthenes would be needed to wage it. In another letter, written in 46, Cicero refers to his own eloquence as *fulmina*, a word usually applied to the oratory of Demosthenes (*Orator* 234; *Letters to Friends* 9.21). Finally Cicero himself refers to his speeches against Antony as "Philippics" (*Letters to Brutus* 2, 4), although in a very informal way, since Aulus Gellius knew them as *orationes Antonianae*.[14]

In any case, in the *Philippics*, beginning with the *Second Philippic*, one sees the first genuine attempt on Cicero's part to imitate Demosthenes' use of style and argumentation. After Antony's furious attack on him in the senate on 19 September, Cicero realized that reconciliation was not possible and that he was engaged in a death struggle to preserve the only form of government in which he himself could function effectively (cf. *Letters to Friends*

12.2, 1). Moreover, Antony had attacked Cicero's whole career, as a politician, as an orator, and as a man; and Cicero realized that his reply had to be a defense of his entire life. Less than two years before, Cicero had put his hand to a Latin translation of Demosthenes' speech *On the Crown*. He had already come to think of himself, both as an orator and as a politician, in terms of Demosthenes. What could be more likely therefore, than that in the defense of his own career he should be deeply influenced by the most famous political defense in Greek oratory, by an orator whom he had come to admire so much and with whom he had begun to identify himself? This is also one reason why the speech was published as a pamphlet: Cicero was embarking on what was almost a rhetorical exercise that he realized might be quite different from the oratory he had practiced all his life. In the treatise *On the Best Kind of Orators*, Cicero says about his translation of the speech *On the Crown*: "Nec converti ut interpres, sed ut orator, sententiis isdem et earum formis tamquam figuris, verbis ad nostram consuetudinem aptis. In quibus non verbum pro verbo necesse habui reddere, sed genus omne verborum vimque servavi. Non ea me adnumerare lectori putavi oportere, sed tamquam appendere" (14). In a very general sense, the *Second Philippic* is a further elaboration of this rhetorical exercise.[15]

There are problems involved in this interpretation, primarily the fact that Cicero does not conceptualize in the *Orator* many of the rhetorical techniques, especially those concerning structure and argumentation, that are most characteristic of Demosthenes and that are found in Cicero's *Philippics* as well. In fact, because of the basic differences between Greek and Latin, the tastes of Roman and Greek audiences, and the personal temperament of Cicero and Demosthenes, these similarities, rather than purely stylistic ones, are the easiest to detect. There are several possible responses to this objection. First, the *Orator* is Cicero's answer to the Neo-Atticists and consequently is primarily a treatise on style, in which there is little discussion of other aspects of oratory. Second, like all ancient critics, Cicero is working within the canons of ancient rhetorical criticism, which do not always correspond to oratorical practices and which, except for style, are not always very helpful in dealing with Demosthenic technique.[16] Third, the *Orator*, which was clearly composed with some haste, was written two years before the publication of the *Second Philippic*; and during that two-year period Cicero surely came to understand more fully the techniques of Demosthenic oratory. This is especially likely if his translation of the speech *On the Crown* was composed after the *Orator*, since in the act of close translation Cicero would come to understand fully the many aspects of Demosthenic oratory that make it so compelling, even if he did not conceptualize those techniques. However, we cannot determine exactly when *On the Best Kind of Orators* was composed or if the translation of the speeches of Aeschines and Demosthenes was ever really done. We do know, nevertheless, that the preface to those translations is roughly contemporary with the *Orator*.[17]

Another problem is that there are very few specific passages in Cicero's *Philippics* in which he seems to be copying Demosthenes closely or verbatim; and this, probably more than any other factor, has discouraged critics who deal with the influence of Demosthenes on these speeches.[18] It is unlikely, however, that an orator as mature and experienced as Cicero would slavishly imitate specific passages; and the comments from *On the Best Kind of Orators* quoted above would support this thesis. What is more probable is that he let himself be inspired, in a more general way, by Demosthenic techniques of developing and presenting themes and arguments; that topic will be discussed in the remainder of this chapter.[19] In any case, it is clear that Cicero had been studying and reading Demosthenes extensively in the two years preceding his conflict with Antony and, like Demosthenes in reference to Athens, he realized that this was one of the fundamental crises in Roman history, a crisis in which the existence of Rome as he knew it and his own place in history was at stake. It is debatable whether the nature of the *Philippics* was determined by this realization and the existence of a pattern of oratory that this sort of crisis always evokes, rather than the direct influence of Demosthenes, or whether it was determined by some combination of the situation and the Demosthenic influence; but this issue will be considered in the last chapter. What is important now is to determine more clearly those traits that characterize Cicero's last speeches and to see whether there are, in fact, parallel techniques used in Demosthenes; we may begin with the *Second Philippic*.

The general approach of this speech and *On the Crown*, which inspired it, is very similar both in tactics and structure. Both Cicero and Demosthenes undercut the arguments of their opponents from the outset by identifying themselves and their policies with the audience before which the speech is delivered, arguing that their honors and their successes have been public honors and national successes. Thus, any attack on Demosthenes or Cicero becomes an attack on the Athenian people or the Roman senate, and vice versa.[20] Also, both evoke sympathy from the audience by pleading the difficulties involved in praising themselves, a task that has been forced on him in each case by the opponent, and promise that they will be moderate and restrained (*On the Crown* 3–4; *Philippic II* 5, 10).

Both orators devote the first long section of their speeches to a defense of their own lives. Each is composed of a brief segment on personal life followed by a more lengthy defense of public policies, which are arranged in chronological order. This portion of the speech shows clearly, once again, the close identification that these orators make between the state and themselves.[21] Each orator thus depicts himself as an outstanding citizen and establishes thereby an atmosphere favorable to himself in preparation for the second part of the speech, which is an attack on his opponent, who becomes the scapegoat for all the troubles that have befallen the state. This part of the speech, like the first, begins with a discussion of the opponent's private life, which is followed by an attack on his public policies.[22] The last section of each speech, preceding the peroration, involves a comparison. Demosthenes compares himself and Aeschines as statesmen (297–323); Cicero compares Caesar and Antony (116–18), with the obvious implication that the fate of the former awaits the latter. Both speeches end in typically Demosthenic, and very un-Ciceronian, fashion, on a calm note, a prayer that the gods will keep the state free. In both speeches there is throughout a mixture of political defense and attack and personal abuse, as well as a typically Demosthenic blend of narrative and characterization, the narrative being used to illustrate the characterization and the characterization showing that the acts of the opponent derive directly from his evil nature.[23]

Moreover, this speech of Cicero contains a repetition of themes or motifs that is truly Demosthenic.[24] Cicero has really outshone his model in this respect, however, for his abilities at varying his basic theme, that his life and career have been beneficial to the state and that Antony's have been detrimental (the appeal to expediency), are even better than those of Demosthenes. Themes such as Cicero's constant opposition to the enemies of the state, Antony's collaboration with those enemies, Cicero's glory and credit that reflect well on the Roman people, and Antony's public and private vices recur throughout the speech in cleverly varied ways, making the impact of the whole speech much more forceful. Both Demosthenes and Cicero argue that it is their actions, not those of their opponents, that have been approved by most people in the state; that it is their opponents who have hired themselves to and cooperated with those who wished to impose slavery on the state; that they have attempted to uphold the past traditions of the state, the finest ideals of Athens and Rome; and that the state has benefited from their advice, which is proved by the singular and unprecedented honors that have been voted to them. Both frequently refer to the past to illustrate that they have maintained in their policies the finest traditions of the state, those ideals that had made the state great in the past; that they were motivated by the same principles that motivated their forefathers, unlike their opponents who were motivated by greed and a basically malicious nature; and that they alone consistently foresaw the best policies for the state.[25]

Cicero, like Demosthenes, also repeats certain images that tend to hold the long speech together and to make its impact more forceful. The image of Antony's vomiting, for example, an image that Cicero may have taken from Demosthenes (cf. *On the Crown* 50), occurs several times in the speech.[26] Another image that Cicero probably took from Demosthenes is the image of buying and selling that recurs throughout the speech.[27] Both orators underline the venality of their opponents by repeating the motif that they have bought and sold in their own interests and to the detriment of the state (cf. *Philippic II*, 98). Cicero also surely took from Demosthenes the image of Antony as the seed from which all the misfortunes of Rome arose.[28]

That Cicero's style really attained its perfection in later years was pointed out long ago by Henry Nettleship. The Demosthenic influence on this later style has also been pointed out, although not always in an explicit way. According to Nisbet: "What gives the *Philippics* their unique quality is their energy. . . . Here at least is some of the true Demosthenic 'rapidity' and purposefulness." Laurand had these comments about the style of the *Philippics*: "Son style est plus pur: et il a laissé tomber les ornements factices. La phrase est imcomparablement plus vigoreuse et plus nette. Au lieu d'une abondance la force."

This description of the style of the *Philippics* of Cicero could be applied equally well to the oratory of Demosthenes, as Galen Rowe has demonstrated.[29]

Ralph Johnson has discussed the evolution of Cicero's style, especially that of the *Philippics*.[30] In his book Johnson does not point out the influence of Demosthenes on the style of Cicero's later speeches; however, his description of that style shows this influence clearly. He de‑scribes this as a style in which "statement predominates over embellishment in a very striking way," a description that could easily apply to Demosthenes.[31] Johnson also brings out clearly that in the later speeches Cicero more than ever is in firm control of his style, which does exactly what it is intended to do and is never used excessively.[32] Style here is a means of persuasion; it is never allowed to control the thought or used simply for decoration, which is also characteristic of Demosthenes.[33] Johnson also points out the greater variety of these speeches, both in style and in the modulation of tone. In a very significant passage, he speaks of a typical sentence from a speech of this period (*Philippic IV*): "It differs from the bad sentences in that style (i.e., the luxuriant, periodic style) only in the firm control of its structure, and it differs from the good sentences in that style only in the fact that in its speech it is the wide exception rather than the rule. The sentences before and after it conform to the common pattern for this later style in being for the most part brief and simple in structure. The elaborate sentence, then, is re‑served for creating a very special emphasis."[34] This again could apply equally well to Demosthenes, who realized that it was more effective to blend his well-constructed periods with sentences of a looser and freer construction and who combined with an expert hand the elaborate and the simple, the periodic and the unperiodic, the strained and the relaxed.[35]

In addition to pointing out that Cicero shows a new fondness for simple or compound sentences over periodic sentences, Johnson also shows that the type of period that he prefers in this late style is the initial or initial-terminal sentence, which states the main clause at the outset and then spins out the ramifications of that thought in the subordinate clauses.[36] This is true of Demosthenes as well, especially in the speech *On the Crown*. Rowe notes Demosthenes' preference for simple sentences, and Ronnet has commented on his preference for the so-called analytical period described above.[37] Johnson sees Cicero's vanity, his desire to replace his old style, which had become "out-worn" and incapable of commanding an audience, as the cause of this change:[38] however, it was surely his newly found admiration for Demosthenes that effected these innovations.

The *Second Philippic*, however, was not delivered. Therefore, any generalizations about its nature are not very conclusive unless they can be substantiated in the other *Philippics*, which were delivered. Let us turn to those speeches to see whether there is Demosthenic influence that can be detected in them.[39]

Chapter 4

The Disjunctive Mode:

Philippics III, IV, V, and *VI*

As pointed out in chapter 1, Cicero and Demosthenes were above all advocates, and this made them prone to stake out clear positions and to defend those positions to the end with every means available. Cicero especially had received an education that emphasized the ability to argue opposite points of view. Both men also realized that they were involved in a struggle for existence, and the will to survive heightened this tendency to see the contests with Philip and Antony as a clear-cut struggle between good and evil.

One of the most striking characteristics, therefore, of the rhetoric of crisis is the clarity and simplicity with which the orator views the situation that he faces. To him the contest is black and white, the struggle of good against evil; and what is at stake, he argues, is the very existence of the civilization that he is defending. He tries to convince the members of his audience that the history of their state has reached a fundamental crisis in which its very existence as they know it and everything that it represents are in danger. He then presents the situation as a clear choice between mutually exclusive and fundamentally opposed systems by means of what may be called the disjunctive mode. This determines many aspects of the orator's style—sentence patterns, arguments, presentation of character, structure of speeches, and images. These bring out and emphasize the unequivocal nature of the situation as the orator sees it. This type of approach is found in both Demosthenes and Cicero's *Philippics*, as can be seen from the preceding discussion of Demosthenes' *On the Crown* and Cicero's *Second Philippic*. In both of these speeches, the main informing principle is the contrast between Demosthenes and Aeschines, on the one hand, and Cicero and Antony, on the other, and the policies and goals that they represent. The same technique, and the Demosthenic influences that helped to produce it, can be illustrated from the next four of Cicero's *Philippics*.

The situations that produced Demosthenes' *Olynthiacs* and Cicero's *Third Philippic* were very similar. In each case, the state was in danger and an unhoped-for opportunity to alleviate that danger was suddenly presented. Philip had attacked Olynthus, which appealed to Athens for help, thus unexpectedly offering Athens a marvelous opportunity for gaining a powerful ally against Philip and a base of operations in the north, if Athens would only act quickly and seize the opportunity. Likewise, Rome was threatened by Antony, who was marching with his legions from Brundisium when suddenly Octavian raised legions against him, two of Antony's legions defected to Octavian, and Decimus Brutus issued an edict barring Antony from his province. This turn of events thus gave the senate, which had been in an impossible situation, the opportunity of rallying loyal Romans against Antony, if it could only act quickly.[1] Also, in a more general way, Cicero, who had been studying Demosthenes intensely, must have realized even more than in the *Second Philippic* that the crisis had arrived and that he was fighting for the very existence of Rome as he knew it, the only type of constitution in which he himself could function effectively. In other words, he must have seen even more clearly the parallel between himself and Demosthenes.[2] It is only natu-

ral, therefore, to assume that Cicero turned to Demosthenes for inspiration in composing the *Third Philippic*
against Antony.[3]

The tone of the speech is urgent, underlining Cicero's
attempt to present the situation as having been reduced to
a basic and final conflict between freedom and tyranny, a
conflict in which the senate must act rapidly if Roman
liberty is to be preserved.[4] The tone is brought out dis-
tinctly in the exordium, which opens with the word *se-
rius* and ends with *celeritatis*, which is here opposed to
the weaker word *festinatio* and put in a most emphatic
position at the end of the last sentence of the exordium.
Cicero's intense efforts ("flagitabam") to rouse the senate
and the fundamental nature of the conflict ("contra aras
et focos, contra vitam fortunasque") reinforce this idea.
The verb *exspectare* or nouns or adjectives formed from it
appears five times in the exordium, and the idea of the
need for haste that it conveys is reinforced by other conventions that give the same sense: "minima dilatio temporis"; "breve tempus est longum imparatis"; "Dies enim
adfert *vel hora potius*, nisi provisum est, magnas saepe
clades"; "simul ut magistratum inierint." The urgency of
the situation is also brought out by the contrast between
war plans, in this case the struggle for existence, and
other functions of the state: "certus autem dies non ut
sacrificiis, sic consiliis exspectari solet." This   an imitation of Demosthenes' *First Philippic* (37).

The need for haste is reflected, moreover, in the very
nature of the exordium, which, although it sets the tone
of the whole speech, is not just an introduction to the
speech but the beginning of the argumentation. In it are
contained most of the major ideas that will be developed
in the speech: Antony's intentions, the need for quick action, the necessity of supporting Decimus Brutus, Octavian, and the consuls-elect in their efforts against Antony. Quite in keeping with the tone of the whole speech,
therefore, Cicero thus gives the impression of being eager
and impatient to get to the topic at hand.

This urgent, almost desperate tone, underlining the need for action before it is too late, is kept up elsewhere in the speech. If, says Cicero, Octavian had not raised an army and marched on Rome, "rem publicam scelere Antonii *nullam* haberemus" (5),[5] and he argues that before the arrival of Octavian "rem publicam *funditus* interituram fuisse" (5). Likewise, alluding to the theme that republican Rome has been snatched from death and reborn, as it were, he argues that the relief felt when Decimus Brutus, the descendant of Lucius, attacked Antony was even greater than that felt when the last king was driven from Rome. The need for quick action by the senate to support Brutus and Octavian is brought out by the repetition of the following phrase, with the verb in the emphatic initial position: "Faciendum est igitur nobis, patres conscripti" (7, 12); and the theme of urgency is picked up again toward the end of the speech: "Hanc igitur occasionem oblatam tenete" (34) and "nunc iam apertum est; omnes patefaciunt, in utramque partem quid sentiant, quid velint" (36). Finally, Cicero's image of himself as goading on a willing Octavian also conveys this need for haste: "Sed tamen currentem, ut dicitur, incitavi" (19).

All of this clearly reflects the *kairos* theme, used so often by Demosthenes in the *Philippics* and especially in the *Olynthiacs*; and he was clearly Cicero's inspiration here.[6] Moreover, the use of a simple exordium that leads directly into the heart of the speech, reflecting the orator's impatience to proceed as quickly as possible to the business at hand, and the repetition of certain key themes, often introduced in the exordium to the speech, are Demosthenic techniques,[7] on which Cicero was surely modeling his own oratory here.

This urgent tone is related to the gravity of the situation as Cicero presents it, a situation in which the choices have been reduced to the most basic. It is clearly reflected in the simplicity of the sentence structure of the most crucial passages in the speech: "Quapropter, quoniam res in id discrimen[8] adducta est, utrum ille poenas rei pub-

licae luat, an nos serviamus" (29). The choice is stated
again toward the end of the speech: "Ad decus et ad liber-
tatem nati sumus; aut haec teneamus aut cum dignitate
moriamur" (36).[9] Indeed, the simple alternative is brought
out most clearly in one of the most unusual similes in all
of Cicero. Although it is usually his enemies who are
compared to gladiators (18, 31), in a simile that makes the
image even more striking through its reversal, Cicero
compares himself and the senate to *gladiatores nobiles*,
who, in a life-and-death struggle, have only one choice:

> Quod si iam (quod di omen avertant!) fatum ex-
> tremum rei publicae venit, quod gladiatores nobiles
> faciunt ut honeste decumbant, faciamus nos, prin-
> cipes orbis terrarum gentiumque omnium, ut cum
> dignitate potius cadamus quam cum ignominia
> serviamus. (35)[10]

The a fortiori argument is evident in the contrast between
gladiatores nobiles and *principes orbis terrarum gen-
tiumque omnium*. This image, like similar ones in Demosthenes, also underlines Cicero's combative nature,
which was discussed in chapter 1.

Such a mutually exclusive disjunctive argumentation is
found elsewhere in this speech. When discussing the actions of Octavian and Antony, Cicero says, "Necesse erat
enim alterutrum esse hostem; nec poterat aliter de adver-
sariis ducibus iudicari" (21), and this type of argument is
used in reference to the legions as well (14). All of this underlines Cicero's attempt to convince his audience that
the choice now facing the senate and Roman people is
simple and clear.[11]

Demosthenes is also fond of presenting the situation as
he perceives it in terms of a simple alternative that affects
the very existence of the Athenian state.[12] In both the
Olynthiacs (cf. *Olynthiac III* 8) and the *Philippics* (cf.
Philippic III 8), he presents Philip as having left the Athenians a simple choice; like Cicero, he presents the choice

as being that between freedom and slavery, between the finest traditions of Athens and subjugation to a tyrant.[13] Moreover, like Cicero, he presents this choice in the simplest and most straightforward terms, reflecting the simplicity of the situation as he sees it. He prefers images of struggle and combat from athletics and hunting because these reflect this struggle for survival,[14] a struggle involving his own survival as an influential politician.

Cicero's portrait of Antony helps to underline the simplicity of the choice facing the Roman people, just as Demosthenes' portrait of Philip shows the Athenians that he is the sort of man with whom they could not possibly cooperate.[15] Cicero depicts Antony from the very beginning of the speech as a hopeless degenerate: "homine profligato ac perdito" (1). His portrait of Antony, however, becomes more intense in the course of the speech. At first he is un-Roman, then he is no Roman, and by the end of the speech he is inhuman. Early in the speech, Cicero emphasizes Antony's cruelty by relating a vivid vignette with the sort of detail that would stick in the hearer's mind, the type of vignette favored by Demosthenes that makes the character of the opponent more "present" to the audience:[16] Antony had ordered the butchery of certain citizens at Brundisium in the home of his host "quorum ante pedes eius morientium sanguine os uxoris respersum esse constabat" (4). Then, using the argument a fortiori, a technique Demosthenes often uses in the *Philippics* (cf. *Philippic III* 35), Cicero asks the senate to imagine (a much more compelling procedure than trying to describe it himself) what measures Antony, "crudelitate imbutus" (4), would have taken against the senate and other "boni," against whom he was "multo . . . iratior quam illis," if Octavian had not rescued Rome. Having illustrated Antony's cruelty, the first element in his description of Antony as being un-Roman, he then proceeds to the second, his tyrannical tendencies and his desire to make the Romans slaves. This is an important leitmotiv in the speech, as it is in the speeches of Demosthenes against Philip. This he accomplishes by a comparison of Decimus Brutus and his ancestor Lucius and their actions against Tarquin and Antony, which leads into a long, and unconvincing, comparison of the latter two in which Tarquin is depicted as being merely proud whereas Antony is impious, tyrannical, and unpatriotic (8–11). Again using the argument a fortiori, he argues that the Roman people's gratitude to Decimus Brutus should consequently be even greater than that of their ancestors to Lucius Brutus. To clinch his argument that Antony has tyrannical leanings, he then relates (12) the episode at the Lupercalia in which Antony offered Caesar a crown, as in the *Second Philippic* (85).

Having established that Antony is un-Roman (he sums up the two ideas supporting this thesis: "intolerabile est servire impuro, impudico, effeminato, numquam ne in metu quidem sobrio"),[17] he then attempts to show that he is no Roman, that by his actions he has become a public enemy, a *hostis* (14).[18] The portrait becomes even more intense, however, for Cicero, as he promises,[19] will ultimately argue that he is not even human, separating him in climactic succession even further from Cicero's audience. Later in the oration, Antony becomes a *beluam* (28), an animal to whom even meaningful speech, the most basic characteristic dividing men from animals, is denied. After citing some of Antony's sayings, Cicero explains: "Quis sic loquitur? . . . Nonne satius est mutum esse quam, quod nemo intellegat, dicere."[20] He then states that Sextus Clodius, Antony's teacher of rhetoric, has done nothing but remove his ability to use speech in a meaningful way: "hominem stupidum magis etiam *infatuet* mercede publica" (22). He is nothing, Cicero argues, but a conglomeration of vices: "Quid est in Antonio praeter libidinem, crudelitatem, petulantiam, audaciam? Ex his totus conglutinatus est. Nihil apparet in eo ingenuum, nihil moderatum, nihil pudens, nihil pudicum" (28). Again, like an animal, he not only cannot use meaningful speech, he is totally dominated by passion.[21] Without a human mind, he "nec ruere demens nec furere desinit" (31).[22]

All of this is quite similar to Demosthenes' portrait of Philip, and that was probably Cicero's inspiration here. Like Philip, Antony is cruel and barbaric; he desires to impose slavery on the Roman people as Philip desired to enslave the Greek states.[23] Antony is like Philip in that he refuses to be discouraged by temporary setbacks or defeats.[24] Cicero depicts Antony as being totally alien to the audience that he is addressing; likewise, Demosthenes isolates Philip from his audience by depicting him as being of totally un-Greek extraction, a barbarian of the worst sort, which to a Greek involved the inability to use speech in a meaningful way.[25] Demosthenes' opponent is a foreigner, but he nevertheless hammers away at the idea that he is not like the Greeks in any way. Cicero's opponent is a noble Roman, but he tries to convince his audience that he is totally foreign to them in every way. In both orators, the depiction of the character of the opponent is among the most compelling of their arguments.

Cicero also develops Antony's character by contrast, just as Demosthenes develops Philip's character by comparing him with the Spartans and the Athenians of former times (cf. *Philippic III* 25–31). In fact, the first fourteen sections of the speech follow a very regular pattern that brings out Antony's character by contrasting him with the loyal elements in the state. This repetition of a basic theme and pattern, the contrast between Antony and loyal Romans, brought out by showing Antony from different points of view, contributes to the directness of the speech, isolates Antony even more, and reinforces the idea of a clear-cut choice. In each section in which this procedure is used, there is praise of a loyal element in the state: Octavian (3–5), the Martian and Fourth Legions (5–8), Decimus Brutus (8–12), and Gaul and the tribunes (12–14). In each case, praise is followed by an attack on Antony, in which he is contrasted with the loyal element.

The praise of the supporter of the state is then repeated in a sort of ring composition, and this is followed by a concrete proposal to the effect that the loyal element should be officially praised and Antony condemned by the senate, thus allowing Cicero to repeat briefly the ideas already expressed. In each of these sections, there is a mixture of narration, argumentation, and proposal. In the first, for example, Octavian is praised (3–6); and this praise is supported by a short narration of his actions in defense of the state. Next Antony is attacked; using an argument a fortiori, Cicero justifies this attack by narrating Antony's actions in Brundisium and predicting what his actions in Rome would have been. He then returns to his praise of Octavian and makes a concrete proposal that his actions should be approved officially by the senate. For clarity, Cicero repeats his basic ideas in summary form at the end of each pattern (cf. sec. 7) and uses clear transitions (cf. the beginning of sec. 8), which also sum up what he has already said and contribute to the directness of the speech through repetition. These patterns are arranged not only in chronological order, according to the time of the actions of each loyal element in the state, but also in a climactic order, increasing their intensity and building up to the summary and the proposal that Antony be declared a public enemy (14), which comes in the center of the speech.[26]

Again, such patterns are quite reminiscent of Demosthenes. Like Cicero in this speech, Demosthenes prefers the repetition of a few basic ideas presented throughout the speech from slightly different points of view and arranged on either side of the center of the speech (the *cardo*), which usually contains the major proposal.[27] Most of Cicero's basic themes, the need to seize the opportunity offered by the gods, the necessity of upholding the traditions of Rome, the fundamental threat to the existence of the state, are Demosthenic.[28] The discussion of these ideas preceding the proposal shows why the proposal is necessary; that following the center of the speech tends to show how the proposal would solve the problems discussed earlier. Likewise, Demosthenes also prefers a combination of argument, refutation and confirmation, and narration sprinkled throughout the speech rather than the linear pattern recommended by the handbooks.[29]

Cicero proceeds similarly here. Having stated his major proposal in the center of the speech, building up to it through the use of a repeated pattern of arguments that seem to justify the need for action, he constructs the rest of the speech in a similar way, repeating, again for emphasis, many of the ideas that preceded the proposal and trying to show how his proposals would solve the problems he had discussed earlier. First, there is a comparison of Octavian and Cicero's nephew, Q. Cicero, with Antony (15–18), which primarily involves praise of Octavian and Q. Cicero and attacks on Antony's background and family, similar to the sort of personal attacks that one often finds in Demosthenes.[30] Cicero again picks up ideas that have already been discussed earlier in the speech. Then he proceeds to an attack on Antony's most recent public acts, which, like those of the republican supporters, are arranged in chronological order:[31] "Sed quid fecit ipse?" (19). This section, broken by an attack on Antony's inability to speak clearly (22), which reinforces the earlier attack on his character, is also arranged in chronological order: the meeting in the senate presided over by Antony on 28 November, Antony's flight from the senate, and the actions in the senate after his departure (19–27). Structured in ring composition like the smaller sections that precede the center of the speech, it too concludes with the praise of Octavian (27). Then Cicero breaks the pattern of praise-attack-praise-proposal (and thus calls attention to this important section of the speech) by inserting between the praise of Octavian and the very formal proposal that concludes the speech (39) one of the most moving sections in Roman oratory, a section that deals with Cicero's political role and repeats many of the ideas already developed in the previous sections of the speech. This optimistic section begins on a hopeful note, brought out by a striking image: "Hodierno die primum, patres conscripti, longo intervallo in possessione libertatis pedem ponimus" (28). Many of the ideas brought out earlier in the speech are then repeated: the reasons for Cicero's attack on Antony, an appeal to basic Roman traditions, a review of Antony's crimes both pubic and private (28–32), the god-given opportunity to reestablish the republic for which Cicero has reserved himself (32–34), the necessity for the senate to seize the opportunity and uphold the traditions of Rome (34–35). Before the proposal at the end, the speech concludes with the urgent tone of the exordium: the time is right for success, the opportunity will not come again.

In addition to those discussed above, there are other elements in this speech that are typically Demosthenic. The rapid change of tone and the wide variety of emotions in the speech (cf. secs. 22, 23, 28) are typical of Demosthenes,[32] as is the tendency, unusual in Cicero, to conclude the speech on a very calm note, with a résumé of the concrete proposals that have been made in the course of it.[33] The cautiously hopeful tone of the end of Cicero's *Third Philippic* is also characteristic of Demosthenes, underlining the theme that is brought out over and over again in both orators that the situation is not hopeless.[34]

The *Fourth Philippic*, which is Cicero's report to the people of what had transpired in the senate earlier in the day, is very similar to the *Third*, both in subject matter and expression. The urgent but hopeful tone of his speech in the senate is brought out clearly in the proemium, in the first sentence of which he speaks of his "alacritatem . . . summam defendendae rei publicae . . . spem recuperandae" (1). He tells the people that the actions of the senate have brought light ("aliquid lucis") to the dark situation shrouding the state[35] and that when he sees the

enthusiasm of the people he is encouraged even more
("Nunc vero multo sum erectior").

The first argument in the body of the speech is a restatement of the disjunctive syllogism, the "black-or-
white" perception of the situation, which is so characteristic of the *Third Philippic*: "Neque enim, Quirites,
fieri potest, ut non aut ii sint impii, qui contra consulem
exercitus comparaverunt, aut ille hostis contra quem iure
arma sumpta sunt" (2). As usual, in the term *iure* Cicero
indicates clearly which half of the syllogism he favors.
Praise of Octavian follows in a magnificent sentence that
opens by calling attention to the uniqueness of the situation, passes through a long series of subordinate clauses
describing the many aspects of the danger that threatened
the state, and ends with the phrase "Antonique furorem
. . . a pernicie rei publicae averteret" (3), thus reflecting
the reality of the situation, the sudden salvation brought
by Octavian at the end. An attack on Antony and a résumé of the decree honoring Octavian follow (4).

Similarly to the *Third Philippic*, Cicero next discusses
the actions of the Martian Legion and repeats the disjunctive syllogism that dominates these speeches: "Nam si
ille non hostis, hos qui consulem reliquerunt hostis necesse est iudicemus" (5). Then comes another attack on
Antony, followed by praise of both legions and their com-
mendation by the senate (6).

Cicero then gives a résumé of his arguments and allows
the people to add their voice to those that condemn Antony. Praise of Brutus follows, with the implication, as in
the *Third Philippic*, that he has been almost the second
founder of the republic. Again he repeats the syllogism:
"Si consul Antonius, Brutus hostis: si conservator rei publicae Brutus, hostis Antonius" (8).[36] This is followed by a
summary of the decrees of the senate and a résumé of the
whole argument about whether Antony is a loyal Roman:
"Negat hoc D. Brutus . . . negat Gallia, negat cuncta Ita-
lia, negat senatus, negatis vos. Quis illum igitur consulem

nisi latrones putant?" (9). Cicero then attacks these followers of Antony and closes this part of the speech on the hopeful note with which it began: the gods will protect Rome, liberty and freedom are near (10).

Then, just as he earlier made an appeal to the senate and discussed the nature of the conflict toward the end of the *Third Philippic,* Cicero here exhorts the Roman people in a similar way. Like Demosthenes, he says that he will act as a commander in a struggle over the very survival of Rome:[37] "Non est vobis, Quirites, cum eo hoste certamen, cum quo aliqua pacis condicio esse possit. Neque enim ille servitutem vestram, ut antea, sed iam iratus sanguinem concupiscit (11). . . . Non est vobis res, Quirites, cum scelerato homine ac nefario, sed cum immani taetraque belua . . . agitur enim, non qua condicione victuri, sed victuri simus an cum supplicio ignominiaque perituri" (12). Also, as in the *Third Philippic,* this is followed by repeated exhortations to the Roman people to live up to the noble ideals and traditions of their ancestors (13 – 14);[38] and the speech ends on an optimistic note, coupled with another reference to the decrees of the senate: "Me auctore et principe ad spem libertatis exarsimus" (15).

Cicero's *Fifth* and *Sixth Philippics* show the same sort of disjunctive reasoning and the same directness as the *Third* and the *Fourth.* Like those speeches, and unlike Cicero's earlier orations, which are sometimes obfuscated, convoluted, digressive, and hesitant,[39] these speeches are clear, clean, decisive, and sure.[40] Again Cicero sees the situation as a simple and clear-cut alternative: either Antony is defeated and the Roman republic will survive or Antony will be victorious and the end of the republic is at hand. Here there is none of the vacillating Cicero, seen often during the years of Caesar's ascendancy, who sees too many sides of a problem to come to a firm decision, none of Cicero the compromiser who tries to appease everyone, none of Cicero the coward who shrinks from taking a strong stand.[41] The sureness of his decision to resist Antony and the simplicity of the basic alternative are reflected, once again, in the types of argument, the structure, and other rhetorical tecnhiques that he uses in these speeches.

The historical situation that produced Cicero's *Fifth Philippic* is quite similar to that which produced Demosthenes' first. On 20 December the senate had, in effect, declared Antony a public enemy. Antony was besieging Decimus Brutus in Mutina, and Octavian was marching to Brutus's relief. The state of all-out war against Antony that Cicero had urged in the *Third* and *Fourth Philippics* seemed imminent. However, when the senate met on 1 January 43 B.C., presided over by the new consuls Hirtius and Pansa, Calenus expressed the opinion that an embassy should be sent to Antony before the state committed itself to open warfare; and this opinion was supported by others. In other words, the senate, which had seemed to favor vigorous action in December, now began to back away and seemed inclined to offer words rather than deeds.

This is not dissimilar to the situation faced by Demosthenes in the *First Philippic*. While Philip was interfering in Thrace and Euboea and harassing Athenian shipping in the Aegean and even landing at Marathon, the Athenians sat idly by, deliberating and discussing what to do (*Philippic I* 6−13); and they offered only words, "armies on paper" (19), with which to combat Philip. Through delays and debates the Athenians always lost the opportunity to act effectively and decisively (36−37, 44). Therefore, Demosthenes' problem in this speech, like Cicero's in the *Fifth Philippic*, was to persuade the Athenians of the need to act quickly and to realize that Philip was their enemy, an enemy with whom negotiation was impossible (50). What both the Athenians and the senate needed to offer was deeds, not words.

The exordium of Cicero's speech, therefore, opens with the urgent tone that is so characteristic of the two previous speeches: "Nihil umquam longius his Kalendis Ianuariis mihi visum est" (1). The contrast between Antony's deeds and the lack of action by the senate, similar to those contrasts between the Athenians and Philip that Demosthenes makes so often, follows in the next sentence; however, also as in Demosthenes, the tone of the next passage is hopeful ("spemque attulit non modo salutis conservandae, verum etiam dignitatis pristinae recuperandae"). Using an image of light, which reflects the "black-or-white" syndrome so characteristic of these speeches ("Hic enim dies vobis . . . *inluxit*"),[42] Cicero proceeds to discuss again the *kairos* theme that is so prominent in the preceding *Philippics*: "haec potestas data est" (2). He then uses another example of the disjunctive syllogism that is so typical of the *Third* and *Fourth Philippics*: the Romans have only one choice, "aut honesta pax aut bellum necessarium" (2). Cicero then passes to the issue at hand on this occasion, whether an embassy should be sent to Antony, in what is like a partition of the speech. This acts as a transition to the first major part of the speech, running from sections 3 to 31, which leads up to the proposal that comes, more or less, in the middle of the speech, at section 31. The tone of this section is indicated by the emphatically placed last word of the partition, which is made even more emphatic by the rejected weaker term and the parenthesis that precedes: "Legatos vero ad eum mittere de quo gravissimum et severissimum iudicium nudius tertius decimus feceritis, non iam levitatis est, sed, ut quod sentio dicam, *dementiae*" (3). Cicero's point, like that of Demosthenes in the *First Philippic* (26–27), is that to try to deal with a man like Antony is an indication of a world gone mad, a world that is distorted and paradoxical, a *mundus perversus*; and to try to convey to his audience the departure from the sensible that he sees, he, like Demosthenes, resorts to a literary technique that was even more congenial to the Romans than to the Greeks: the satiric mode.[43]

Now, the object of the satirist is to point out the faults and weaknesses of society; and he uses exaggerated situations to try to shock his audience into a realization that something is wrong. In order to make his attacks more immediate and more vivid to his audience and to convey an air of spontaneity appropriate to an outburst provoked by anger and indignation, his satires are lively and dramatic, relying on the use of dialogue, emotional outbursts, a succession of rather isolated and often rambling discussions, and sudden transitions and digressions. The satirist tries to make members of the audience feel and see what he is attacking in order to arouse in them the same sort of anger that he himself feels.

This is exactly the technique that Demosthenes uses in the *First Philippic* in an attempt to make the Athenians realize the errors of their ways. He presents an image of fourth-century Athens as an irrational and topsy-turvy world, a world in which wars are fought with paper armies, where generals are like clay puppets, where soldiers risk their lives in the courtroom but not on the battlefield. To do so he employs those techniques that are usually associated with satire, strong metaphors and similes that convey the distorted nature of the situation he describes (e.g., Athens is like a Persian boxer); the irony of extreme obviousness to show the departure from normal standards; the alternation between sensible ideals and ridiculous realities, presented through the special rhetoric of satire, paradox, antithesis, caricature, repetition, and imaginary dialogue—all of these making the presentation of the confused and fantastic situation more effective and dramatic. As Galen Rowe points out: "Demosthenes is not satisfied with presenting merely the inanity of the situation; he must further distort the image to the point of absurdity."[44]

This is also the technique that Cicero uses in the first

half of the *Fifth Philippic*. The section begins rather
calmly by restating the major argument of the two preceding speeches: either Antony or those who have taken up
arms against him is an enemy of the state. Cicero soon
becomes more animated, however, at the thought of the
incongruity of the situation:

> Quid? legio Martia, quid? quarta cur laudatur? Si
> enim consulem suum reliquerunt, vituperandae
> sunt, si inimicum rei publicae, iure laudantur. (4)

Cicero's impatience becomes greater as he expands on the
paradoxical nature of the situation:

> Placet eodem tempore praemia constituere eis qui
> contra Antonium arma ceperunt et legatos ad Antonium mittere? ut iam pudendum sit honestiora
> decreta esse legionum quam senatus: si quidem
> legiones decreverunt senatum defendere contra Antonium, senatus decernit legatos ad Antonium. (4)

The contrast between "arma" and "legatos" and the repeated antithesis of "contra Antonium" and "ad Antonium" underline the incongruity of the situation.

Cicero, like Demosthenes (*Philippic I* 49–50), then
passes to the rumors that are circulating in Rome, which
serve only to heighten the ridiculousness of the situation.
At the thought that a decree may be proposed to assign
Antony Further Gaul, Cicero becomes even more animated and sarcastic:

> Quid est aliud omnia ad bellum civile hosti arma largiri, primum nervos belli, pecuniam infinitam qua
> nunc eget, deinde equitatum quantum velit? Equitatum dico? Dubitabit, credo, gentis barbaras secum
> adducere. (5)

Like Demosthenes,[45] he sprinkles these sarcastic outbursts with moral judgments, keeping up the contrast between the sensible expectation and the ridiculous reality
and continuing to underline the disjunctive nature of his

argumentation in these speeches: "Hoc qui non videt, excors, qui, cum videt, decernit, impius est" (5). Also like Demosthenes (cf. *Philippic I* 10–11, 25–26), his indignation builds up to an emotional outburst that takes the form of an imaginary dialogue:

> Nullae istae excusationes sunt: "Meus amicus est." Sit patriae prius. "Meus cognatus." An potest cognatio proprior ulla esse quam patriae in qua parentes etiam continentur? "Mihi pecuniam tribuit." Cupio videre qui id audeat dicere. (6)

After this emotional outburst, he returns to a calm restatement of the issue at hand, as Demosthenes usually does (cf. *Philippic I* 10–12), again bringing out its disjunctive nature: "Agitur utrum M. Antonio facultas detur opprimendae rei publicae, caedis faciendae bonorum, urbis, agrorum suis latronibus condonandi, populum Romanum servitude opprimendi, an horum ei facere nihil liceat" (6). Again as in Demosthenes (cf. *Philippic I* 19–20), this long sentence is followed by a short one that comments on it ("Dubitate quid agatis"); and the argumentation, which becomes heated again, is introduced by an imaginary objection ("'At non cadunt haec in Antonium'").

  This objection is answered by a long series of rhetorical questions and exclamations concerning laws passed by Antony (7–9), which, as is only proper in an emotional outburst, show little transition and are jerky and seemingly unconnected:

> Possuntne hae leges esse ratae sine interitu legum reliquarum? Eccui potestas in forum insinuandi fuit? Quae porro illa tonitrua, quae tempestas! (8)

In this section Cicero continues to underline, by drawing attention to the obvious, the irony and incongruity of the situation:

> Ut, si auspicia M. Antonium non moverent, sustinere tamen eum ac ferre posse tantam vim tem-

> pestatis, imbris, turbinum *mirum* videretur. Quam
> legem igitur se augur dicit tulisse non modo tonante
> Iove sed prope caelesti clamore prohibente, hanc du-
> bitabit contra auspicia latam confiteri? (8)

By exaggeration and caricature, Cicero shows the incredible nature of the situation that Antony has created in
Rome.

Then, like Demosthenes, who likes to present a situation first in the outrageous terms of comedy and satire
and then more calmly (cf. *Philippic I* 25–29), Cicero discusses Antony's laws in a much more logical section
(9–10). Even here, however, a simile underlines the irrational, perverted, and topsy-turvy nature of the world that
Antony has created in Rome. Antony, the consul, keeps
the tribunes and the people out of the forum as if he were
defending a city against the enemy: "Sic vero erant dis-
posita praesidia ut quo modo hostium aditus urbe prohi-
bentur castellis et operibus, ita ab ingressione fori populum tribunosque plebis propulsari videres" (9).

With no logical transition Cicero then passes to an attack on Antony's squandering of public funds and sale of
favors (11–12). Here too Cicero hammers away at the
incredible and almost fantastic nature of the situation
("portenti simile"); and he uses the weapons of satire, exaggerated narration, and description and vivid language.
Business was glowing ("Calebant . . . nundinae") at Antony's house. His wife was auctioning provinces and king-
doms. Decrees of the senate were forged and entered at
the treasury, and all this was done in the presence of foreigners. Cicero concludes the section with the sort of exaggeration that is typical of this part of the speech:

> Quibus rebus tanta pecunia una in domo coacervata
> est ut, si hoc genus pecuniae iure redigatur, non sit
> pecunia rei publicae defutura. (12)

The absurdity of the situation becomes even more intense as Cicero proceeds to a discussion of Antony's juries

(12–18), just as the images in Demosthenes' *First Philip-pic* become more outrageous, building up to the descrip-tion, at the end of the speech, of the generals who risk their life in court but not on the battlefield (47). It is in this section that the world Antony has created in Rome becomes most apparent. It is a world where roles are re-versed, where nothing is in its proper place, where the *mundus perversus* is most obvious. Antony has appointed criminals and foreigners to the juries:

> Cydam amo Cretensem, portentum insulae, homi-nem audacissimum et perditissimum. Sed fac non esse: num Latine scit? num est ex iudicum genere et forma? num, quod maximum est, leges nostras mo-resve novit? num denique homines? Est enim Creta vobis notior quam Roma Cydae. Dilectus autem et notatio iudicum etiam in nostris civibus haberi solet; Cortynium vero iudicem quis novit aut quis nosse potuit? (13)

In this section the techniques of satire are again em-ployed; vivid and outrageous descriptions of particular in-cidents, such as the Greek who excuses himself from jury service according to Athenian law; role reversal, as in the case of the man who is "modo palliati, modo togati"; un-expected conclusions, such as the comment that two men would work well together on the juries since they are fel-low gamblers; and the absurd, such as the jurymen who excuse themselves because they have been exiled and have thus undergone a change of residence. The language is also that of satire, being full of rhetorical questions, ex-clamations, extreme compression, and abrupt transitions:

> Qui porro ille consessus, di boni! Cretensis iudex is-que nequissimus. Quem ad modum ad hunc reus adleget, quo modo accedat? Dura natio est. At Athe-nienses misericordes. (14)

The description becomes even more perverse, however. In addition to the jurors who are known, there are also danc-

ers and harp players ("saltatores, citharistas, totum denique comissationis Antonianae chorum"); and Cicero concludes with the sort of ironic and unexpected twist that is
typical of satire (cf. the end of Juvenal's *Seventh Satire*):

> En causam cur lex tam egregia tamque praeclara
> maximo imbri, tempestate, ventis, procellis, tur-
> binibus, inter fulmina et tonitrua ferretur, ut eos
> iudices haberemus quos hospites habere nemo
> velit. (15)

Cicero concludes this section typically, with a calm résumé of his argument (end of 16).

He then turns to a discussion of Antony's use of armed
guards and to his recent actions, still maintaining the image of the *mundus perversus* that he has created (17–25).
Antony goes around Rome accompanied by gladiators and
barbarian archers (18). He has turned the temple of Con-
cord into a prison ("de templo carcerem fieri"), and armed
brigands move about the house as the senators deliberate
(18). The caricature is carried even further. Antony de-
claims only to provoke a thirst (19), and after days of practice he vomits a speech against Cicero ("atque in me ab-
sentem orationem ex ore impurissimo evomuit"). The
drinking image is kept up: Antony would like to wet his
sword with Cicero's blood (20), and his brother was thirst-
ing for the blood of the orator ("sanguinem nostrum si-
tiebat"). Indeed, this "imagistic texture" is also characteristic of the satiric mode,[46] as is the fairly ridiculous
comparison of Antony and Hannibal (25).

Finally, after a brief narration of Antony's recent acts,
similar to that in the preceding two speeches, Cicero
comes to the point of all this outrageous description: "Ad
hunc, di boni! legatos mitti placet?" (25). This is followed
by a calm argument, based on the inexpediency of delay,
in which Cicero returns to motifs developed earlier in the
speech, combining them in a sort of ring composition:
"Non est verbis rogandus, cogendus est armis (26). . . . ad
nostrum civem mittimus, ne imperatorem, ne coloniam

populi Romani oppugnet" (27). Like Demosthenes (*Philippic I* 12, 49), he makes the point that it is citizens within the state who are most responsible for Rome's problems (32 and 5–6), that this crisis is really an internal as much as an external problem. The argument concludes with a proverb of sorts, as Demosthenes often does (cf. *Philippic I* 47): "Omne malum nascens facile opprimitur: inveteratum fit plerumque robustius" (31).

All of this builds up to Cicero's proposal in the center of the speech ("Quam ob rem, patres conscripti . . ."). Like Demosthenes (cf. *Philippic I* 16–22), he proposes concrete measures to be taken (31) and argues (32) that any *action* on the senate's part will give Antony reason for hesitation (cf. *Philippic I* 17). Then, also like Demosthenes (*Philippic I* 37–38), he quotes a letter of Antony to reinforce his portrait of him (33).

The style of this section, like that of many parts of these speeches, especially the most crucial ones, is unusually simple, straightforward, and direct, more Demosthenic than Ciceronian:

> Sed hoc minus vereor: sunt alia quae magis timeam et cogitem. Numquam parebit ille legatis. Novi hominis insaniam, adrogantiam; novi perdita consilia amicorum, quibus ille est deditus. . . . Sit per se ipse sanus, quod numquam erit: per hos esse ei tamen non licebit. Teretur interea tempus; belli apparatus refrigiscent. (29–30)

There are Demosthenic turns of phrase as well:

> Cum hoc, patres conscripti, bello, bello, inquam, decertandum est, idque confestim; legatorum tarditas repudianda est. (33)

The hyperbaton in splitting the "hoc" from the "bello" and the epanadiplosis in "bello, inquam," both used to call attention to the key word *bello*, the addition of an adverb at the end that further refines the thought,[47] and the short second sentence summing up what has already been said are all typically Demosthenic devices that make the thought clear and direct (cf. *Philippic III* 70).

Cicero then turns to the honors that are to be decreed to the supporters of the state. Just as the section that precedes the proposal not to send an embassy to Antony is written in a low, often comic style and is often presented in a jerky and disconnected way, this section is written in the elevated style of panegyric and is presented in an orderly and very regular manner. The subsections concern Brutus (35–37), Lepidus (38–41), Octavian (42–51), and L. Egnatuleius and the legions (52–53). In each one Cicero presents an argument, then a formal proposal, and then a résumé of the argument; and reflecting the traditional Roman view of *auctoritas*, he follows an order that reflects the position of each man in the hierarchy of the state (35).[48] The style of this section is the "beautiful" style, the stately style usually associated with Cicero, and is filled with sentiments such as disinterested public service, which are appropriate to panegyric:

> Neque enim ullam mercedem tanta virtus praeter hanc laudis gloriaeque desiderat; qua etiam si careat, tamen sit se ipsa contenta: quamquam in memoria gratorum civium tamquam in luce posita laetetur. (35)

The sentiments that move these loyal Romans are traditional Roman attitudes such as hatred of tyranny and slavery (cf. 38) and rivalry in benefiting the state (48), and they are described in copious and regularly developed Ciceronian periods:

> Nihil est illi re publica carius, nihil vestra auctoritate gravius, nihil bonorum virorum iudicio optatius, nihil vera gloria dulcius. (50)

The noble tone of the latter half of the speech is also reflected in the calm and simple peroration, which is really just a brief résumé of what has already been said and a repetition of the need for haste ("Celeritate autem opus est").

In other words, this is the obverse of the *mundus perversus* that Cicero has presented earlier, the praise of loyal elements in the state corresponding to the vituperation of those who attempt to undermine it. As Rowe says in speaking of Demosthenes' *First Philippic*: "'Shame' and 'honor' . . . reveal at the conclusion of the image the persuasive function of Demosthenes' satiric mode. Through satire's double vision the aberration of the present is refuted and the realistic action of the future, embodied by Demosthenes' proposal, is enhanced."[49] Through the juxtaposition of *vituperatio* and *laus*, Cicero and Demosthenes demonstrate to their audience the "senseless lack of realism"[50] of the situation that they find in Athens and Rome. Moreover, like Demosthenes,[51] Cicero uses the base and the elevated as modes of persuasion. Antony's greed, his drunkenness, his concern with the belly, his corruption and sickness (cf. 17, 43), his insanity (37)—all relegate him to the world of satire and comedy,[52] a world where things are not in their proper place, a world that is disordered and perverse; and this is reflected in the style. Loyal Romans, on the other hand, are in a more elevated world, a world more like that which one sees in tragedy, nobly struggling for exalted goals in keeping with the finest traditions of the fatherland. Thus the disjunction in this speech between the low and the elevated, the comic and the tragic, appearing on either side of Cicero's proposal and highlighting that proposal, reflect and focus, once again, the presentation of a basic, mutually exclusive choice that is so characteristic of the *Philippics*. At the risk of appearing fanciful, I would even venture to say that the modulation of tone in this speech, from the incongruous and disjointed description of Antony's activities, to the direct and straightforward language of Cicero's proposal, and finally to the sublimity and regularity of the panegyric section at the end, reflects the transition that

Cicero argues could be accomplished if his advice were taken, a transition from the chaos of the present situation to the reestablishment of those attitudes and traditions that had made Rome great and that would save her once again.

Cicero's *Sixth Philippic*, delivered before the people on 4 January, has the same relationship to the *Fifth* as the *Fourth* does to the *Third*. In this speech Cicero reports to the people what had gone on in the senate during the previous four days, and the speech is very similar in outline and themes to the one that he had delivered in the senate on 1 January.

The first part of the speech (1–3) gives background material. Cicero explains to the people that the senate had decided on 20 December that as soon as the new consuls took office on 1 January they should put to the senate the question of the general state of affairs in the republic and that when they did so he had proposed that a state of tumult be decreed. Although he was enthusiastically supported, he continues, the senate eventually decided, after four days of debate, to send an embassy to Antony to ascertain what his intentions were. The rest of the speech follows the *Fifth Philippic* in general outline.

Cicero first explains the incongruity of sending ambassadors to a man like Antony: "Ad quem enim legatos?" (3). The portrait of Antony here resembles the comic-satiric one that we found in the previous speech; it is presented in the same exaggerated language and often builds up to the same sort of anticlimactic and unexpected conclusion:

> Semper eo tractatus est quo libido rapuit, quo levitas, quo furor, quo vinolentia; semper eum duo dissimilia genera tenuerunt, leonum et latronum; ita domesticis stupris, forensibus parricidiis delectatur ut mulieri citius avarissimae paruerit quam senatui populoque Romano. (4)

Cicero continues the quest for the "bizarre effect" that is usually associated with comedy and satire and that relegates Antony to the realm of the base and the mean.[53] In addition to underlining his greed, his demeaning pursuits, and his inability to control his passions, he is associated with disease and sickness ("pestifera flamma") through the strong metaphorical language of satire and is also described in animal terms ("importunissima belua"),[54] as in previous speeches; and Cicero keeps up the outrageous description, almost a parody of history, of Antony as a second Hannibal ("tamquam Hannibali initio belli Punici denuntiaret" [6]).

In the description of Antony's companions and supporters (9–15), Cicero once again underlines the irrational and incongruous nature of the world that he had identified with Antony in the preceding speech. Antony's brother Lucius, the "Asiatic gladiator," is said to have threatened Antony with death when his resolve was weakening and then is compared to P. Scipio Africanus, the conqueror of Hannibal (10); the description then becomes even more disjointed and irrational. Lucius is said to have more influence with Antony than even Titus Plancus, who was exiled from Rome and then crept back into the city "ita maestus . . . ut retractus, non reversus videretur" (10). In the very next sentence, however, Cicero says that Plancus is an object of Antony's hatred, a man whom he hates as if he were an exile, which he had been, seemingly because he had participated in the burning of the senate house after Clodius' funeral (10), none of which makes any sense at all.[55] Antony's fickleness is then underlined again in the next sentence: "Nam Trebellium valde iam diligit: oderat tum" (11). In addition to these swift reversals, the imagistic language of comedy and satire continues. Trebellius became the apple of Antony's eye ("fert in oculis") once he realized that Trebellius could not manage without a general cancellation of debts; and Trebellius is called "Fide" because, Cicero supposes, he cheats his creditors ("fraudare creditores, domo profugere, propter aes alienum ire ad arma"). The absurd diminutive and affectionate language that Cicero uses with Trebellius is then applied, with great sarcasm and irony, to Lucius, "amores deliciasque vestras" (12). An imaginary dialogue underlines the ridiculousness involved in Lucius's claim to be the patron of the Roman people, as does the absurdity of the "proof":

> Negatis? Num quisnam est vestrum qui tribum non habeat? Certe nemo. Atqui illum quinque et triginta tribus patronum adoptarunt. Rursus reclamatis? Aspicite illam a sinistra equestrem statuam inauratam, in qua quid inscriptum est? "QUINQUE ET TRIGINTA TRIBUS PATRONO." Populi Romani *igitur* est patronus L. Antonius. (12)

The incongruity of the situation is further brought out by the assertion that Lucius claims to be patron of all, although no one would have him as client (12), and the assumption that it must have been his exploits as a gladiator in Asia that led him to have such a high opinion of himself: "Tantumne sibi sumpsit, quia Mylasis myrmillo Thraecem iugulavit, familiarem suum?" (13). The ridiculous description and figurative language continue. By giving away land in Italy, Lucius gained influence with various groups until nothing remained but the Campus Martius, which he would also have distributed if he had not been put to flight (14); however, now that the senate has appealed these land laws, "friget patronus Antonius" (14).

Then, as in the preceding speech, having sketched out the character of the opponent in the most ludicrous terms ("non alienum fuit personas quasdam a vobis recognosci, ut quibuscum bellum geretur" [16]), Cicero returns to an elevated description of his own actions and those of the senate:

> [Ego sum] qui viginti iam annos bellum geram cum impiis civibus. Quam ob rem, Quirites, consilio

> quantum potero, labore plus paene quam potero, excubabo vigilaboque pro vobis. (17–18)

He ends with an exalted contrast between freedom and slavery that is so characteristic of these speeches:

> Venit tempus, Quirites. . . . Populum Romanum servire fas non est, quem di immortales omnibus gentibus imperare voluerunt. Res in extremum est adducta discrimen; de libertate decernitur. Aut vincatis opportet . . . aut . . . serviatis. (19)

The last sentence of the speech sums up his thought and ends with the key word in all these speeches:

> Aliae nationes servitutem pati possunt, populi Romani est propria *libertas*.

As can be seen in the passages just quoted, the most crucial thoughts here, as in the preceding speech, are written in the direct and simple style:

> Mora est adlata bello, non causa sublata (1). . . . Succurrendum est D. Bruto, omnes undique copiae conligendae; moram exhibere ullam in tali cive liberando sine scelere non possumus (7). . . . Ad hunc utrum legatos an legiones ire opportebat? Sed praeterita omittamus: properent legati, quod video esse facturos; vos saga parate (9). . . . Celeritas detracta de causa est; boni tamen aliquid accessit ad causam. (15)

By these various means, as in the preceding speech, Cicero continues to focus his audience's attention on the clear-cut and fundamental nature of the conflict that faces them.

It has been said that "the individual sentences that an author characteristically uses are a good place to begin to search for devices that will constitute, in the round, that writer's technique."[56] The basic antithesis in *Philippics V* and *VI*, the disjunctive contrast between Antony and his followers and loyal Romans, which determines the organization of these speeches as a whole is very much like the disjunctive sentences which we find so often in *Philippics III* and *IV*. One could argue, in fact, that *Philippics V* and *VI* are disjunctive syllogisms "writ large."

I should point out finally that many of the procedures described above are common to Roman invective and are seen in Cicero's earlier speeches, especially the *Verrines* and the *Catilinarians*. Cicero brings forth criticisms of social background and charges of immorality and avarice in order to establish an argument of probability based on character; by these devices he attempts to isolate the opponent. He further heightens this isolation by using animal names such as those found in reference to Verres, Catiline, Clodius, and Piso.[57] It is only in the *Philippics*, however, that one finds these techniques crystallized into what could be called a "mode," as opposed to scattered passages springled throughout the speech. I would argue that the influence of Demosthenes persuaded Cicero to make a more sustained and deliberate use of these techniques than he had done before.

Chapter 5

La Rapide Simplicité de Démosthènes:

Philippic VII

Cicero's *Seventh Philippic* is undoubtedly the finest of his speeches against Antony. It was not occasioned by any particular crisis or topic for discussion, and this gave Cicero the opportunity to deal with the problem of Antony in general and to explore its far-reaching consequences. He thus restated many of the themes and revised many of the techniques that one sees in *Philippics III* through *VI*. An analysis of this speech, therefore, is quite an appropriate sequel to the discussion of the preceding speeches, for we see in it Cicero's ability to rework material that he had already elaborated into a tightly structured and well-organized whole that is a compelling statement of the situation as it had developed to that point.

During the absence of the envoys, whose mission Cicero had announced to the people in the *Sixth Philippic*, Antony had continued to besiege Brutus in Mutina. In Rome, meanwhile, his supporters had begun to circulate rumors to the effect that Antony had moderated his stands and was willing to compromise. The senate, however, had suspended discussion of the issue until the return of the envoys and had turned its attention to other matters. At some time in January, the senate was convened to discuss certain routine matters concerning the Appian Way, the mint, and the Luperci. When Cicero was called upon to express his opinion, he dismissed the topics of debate, a

procedure that was within the traditions of senatorial procedure at least since the time of Cato the Elder, and turned
to a general discussion of the problem of Antony. In its
use of themes and its development of arguments, the *Seventh Philippic* is surely the most Demosthenic of Cicero's
speeches against Antony.[1]

One of the most striking characteristics of Demosthenes' oratory is the simple directness and speed of the
argumentation, the "rapide simplicité de Démosthènes"
pointed out by Fénelon in 1716: "Je les admire tous deux.
Mais je préférois la rapide simplicité de Démosthènes à
la majestueuse abondance de Cicéron." Hugh Blair was
doubtlessly thinking of this trait when he remarked in
1783: "Demosthenes triumphed over all his opponents;
because he spoke always to the purpose, affected no insig-
nificant parade of words, used weighty arguments, and
showed them [his audience] clearly where their interest
lay." Likewise, as a modern critic has demonstrated, one
sees in Demosthenes' mature speeches "a greater directness of argument, a greater speed in the flow of language,
and the absence of any appearance of hesitation."[2]

One of the real secrets of his oratory is his ability to
limit himself to a discussion of only the most crucial arguments and not to crowd in too many points or details,
which often obscure the main lines of the argumentation
and thus make the speech less effective.[3] Moreover, as
Pearson points out, "each paragraph is limited in its appli-
cation; there is no effort to make more than one point at a
time."[4] This ability to treat topics clearly, discretely, and
economically, focusing on what is truly important, contributes as much as anything to the directness and energy
of his speeches. They are flesh, and bones, and muscle.
There is no fat. Galen Rowe reveals that, in spite of the
speed of the argumentation, "Demosthenes proceeds in
an orderly manner from one topic to the next. He is careful, moreover, to indicate the major divisions and digres-

sions of his discourse."[5] In addition, in the various topics that he treats there is a certain amount of repetition or recurrence of ideas from topic to topic, what Rowe calls "a subtle process of elaboration and development"[6] of the basic themes. This elaboration of certain basic ideas at various points throughout the speech also contributes to its directness. Repetition or recurrence becomes a "moyen de persuasion habile et efficace."[7]

It is this same ability to concentrate on the most important arguments, to develop those arguments economically and clearly, to move without hesitation from one point to the next, while holding the whole speech together through the repetition and elaboration of certain basic ideas throughout the discourse, that makes Cicero's *Seventh Philippic* so Demosthenic in nature. Moreover, in this speech, as in the other *Philippics*, there are certain basic themes and approaches to argumentation as well as certain fundamental uses of style that were probably inspired by Demosthenes.

Like many of Demosthenes' speeches (cf. *Olynthiac III*), Cicero's *Seventh Philippic* really has no proemium. As one critic has said in speaking of *Philippic XII*, it is "un discours bloc, sans exorde ni peroraison, fait de points successifs plutôt qu'enchaînés, quoique assez bien séparés."[8] Cicero dismisses the topic of debate very briefly, and with no apology; and the rapidity with which he does so indicates and conveys to the audience his anxiety over the problem of Antony in the north:

> Parvis de rebus sed fortasse necessariis consulimur.
> . . . Quarum rerum etsi facilis explicatio videtur,
> tamen animus aberrat a sententia suspensus curis
> maioribus. (1)

This approach to the topic, indicating the discrepancy between the orator's own thoughts and what is being discussed by others, may well have been inspired by a similar passage at the beginning of Demosthenes' *Third Olynthiac*, where it is also used to indicate the orator's impatience:

> The same thoughts do not occur to me, gentlemen of Athens, when I consider the situation, on the one hand, and the speeches that I hear, on the other. (1)

In both cases the orator presents himself as being different from the other politicians, not only in his greater concern for the situation, but in his greater insight into the crisis that it has reached. Neither Demosthenes nor Cicero, however, dwells upon this difference. That is not important or significant. What is crucial is the situation at hand, the crisis that faces the state; and that is what each orator turns his attention to immediately. Cicero says in the fourth sentence of the speech (and the first three are quite short): "Adducta est enim, patres conscripti, res in maximum periculum et in extremum discrimen." Likewise, Demosthenes points out in the second sentence of the *Third Olynthiac*: "I see that the speeches concern the punishment of Philip, but that the situation has reached a point at which we must consider, rather, how we will avoid disaster ourselves." Both orators make it clear, at the very beginning of their speeches, that the major issue is the tremendous danger that the state faces.

Cicero then turns immediately (secs. 1–8) to an exposition of the situation, which is exactly the approach Demosthenes usually takes in his speeches: "And instead of immediately contrasting his own views or his own attitude with those of others, he proceeds to explain the political situation. . . . It is the facts, the political situation that must be explained; it is no fault of the rank and file of the assembly that they have not understood what is going on; positive explanation has taken the place of self-praise and criticism of rival politicians."[9] Indeed, in Cicero's speech the concern with the situation and "the absence of any attempt to present himself as different from the others or to draw attention to himself,"[10] unusual in Cicero, is even more pronounced than in the Greek orator. Moreover, Cicero does not make his own opinion about the situation clear (sec. 9) until he has carefully and clearly explained the situation in Italy. Demosthenes uses the same approach: "He is speaking only because he has no alternative, because no one else has found a satisfactory answer to the problem of the day; and without any hint at the beginning that he has found the right answer, he begins by explaining the situation and its dangers; the solution does not come until, as in a forensic speech, narrative and argument have prepared the ground."[11] Cicero here uses the same Demosthenic technique of relying on narration and argumentation to prepare the audience to receive the specific proposal at hand and then returning to arguments that support that proposal in the latter part of the speech, a technique that we have seen elsewhere in the *Philippics*.

In the part of the speech leading up to the proposal, we also see Demosthenic techniques. Cicero opens this segment with a Demosthenic pattern for beginning a section of argumentation: a statement of an opinion, a question, and an answer to that question (cf. Dem. *Philippic II* 6):

> Non sine causa legatorum istam missionem semper timui, numquam probavi: quorum reditus quid sit adlaturus ignoro; exspectatio quidem quantum adferat languoris animis quis non videt? Non enim se tenent ei qui senatum dolent ad auctoritatis pristinae spem revirescere. (1)

The answer to his question is pure Demosthenes. In it Cicero makes the contrast between the "languor" of loyal Romans, what Demosthenes calls "rhathumia," and the activity of their opponents. Demosthenes says in the *Second Olynthiac*:

> It is no wonder that Philip, if he campaigns actively and shares himself the toils of battle and is present

>   at them all and takes advantage of every season and
>   every opportunity, gets the best of us, who delay and
>   pass decrees and ask questions. (23)

In the sentences of both Demosthenes and Cicero, the
active antagonist is described in the indicative verb but
the passive victim is appropriately depicted in a subordinate construction, an infinitive in Latin and a participle
in Greek. Both orators, in keeping with the basically
optimistic and appropriately encouraging tone of their
speeches, also make it clear that it is not resources but
action that is needed. Cicero points out clearly the resources of the senate in its conflict with Antony: "con-
iunctum huic ordini populum Romanum, conspirantem
Italiam, paratos exercitus, expeditos duces" (1). Likewise,
Demosthenes argues in the *Third Olynthiac* (cf. also
Dem. *Philippic III* 40): "Therefore, action must be added;
we have enough of everything else" (15).

Cicero continues the argumentation with another Demosthenic technique for leading into a discussion, an explanation of the rumors that are circulating and how he
would answer them:

>   Iam nunc fingunt responsa Antoni eaque defen-
>   dunt. (2)

Demosthenes also repeatedly argues that it is deeds, not
rumors, that determine how a situation must be viewed:

>   For the rumormongers are the most foolish of all.
>   But if putting aside these rumors we see that the
>   man is our enemy and that he is stripping us of our
>   possessions and has wronged us for a long time . . .
>   then we shall have reasoned rightly. (*Philippic I* 50)

The phrase *fingunt responsa* that Cicero uses is, in fact,
very similar to the term λογοποιοῦντες in Demosthenes.
Likewise, as in Demosthenes (cf. *Philippic III* 14), there
is also in Cicero the clear implication that the rumormongers are in the pay of the adversary, which is made

clear by the fact that they defend the responses that they have invented.[12] Like Demosthenes also (cf. *Philippic II* 13–16), Cicero then methodically refutes each of these rumors by means of sarcasm and irony (2–3). All of this leads up to the accusation that these rumormongers, who are now specifically referred to as "quasi providi cives et senatores diligentes" and whom Cicero will later brand as "improbi," make against Cicero, namely, that he is a warmonger. As Taddeo says of this passage: "The reference to these people as 'quasi providi' only heightens the importance which Cicero puts on the *providere* theme, which he has indisputably reserved for himself, as evidenced in his *Second Philippic*. Thirdly, by having himself referred to as 'bellicus,' he assumes a defensive position, as it would seem. Actually, all he is doing is isolating himself, as Demosthenes does so often, from the rest of the body politic in order to illustrate how in the end, he only had the right advice and thus truly can claim the title of 'providus.'"[13] This attempt to isolate himself is very similar to the beginning of the speech.

Moreover, Cicero dramatizes the argument of his opponents by introducing what might be their direct words with a direct question:

> Nonne sic disputant? "Inritatum Antonium non oportuit." (3)

Demosthenes is quite fond of the same procedure:

> "But by Zeus," someone would say on the grounds that he knows these things well, "he did not do these things from ambition . . . but because the Thebans made juster claims than you." (*Philippic II* 13)

This technique adds liveliness to the argument and helps contribute to the directness of the speech.

Like Demosthenes, Cicero also concludes this section of the preliminary argument with a thought cast in the form of a gnomic expression or proverb (cf. *Philippic I* 50; *Philippic III* 5). It reflects a common Demosthenic theme, that the real problem is an internal one, those enemies within the state, and that these must be punished before other problems can be dealt with:

> Utrum igitur in nefariis civibus ulciscendi, cum possis, an pertimescendi diligenter cautio est? (3)

Demosthenes often expresses the same thought:

> You must hate those who speak on his behalf, considering that it is not possible to overcome the enemies of the city, until you punish those in the city itself who serve them (*Philippic III* 53).

Finally, as if to call attention to the Demosthenic inspiration of this passage, as he sometimes does,[14] Cicero uses an expression that is very unusual in Latin and is probably modeled on a similar expression in Demosthenes. He says that the rumormongers argue that there are men even more wicked than Antony against whom the state must beware. Cicero's comment on this is: "quos quidem a se primum numerare possunt" (3). The phrase *a se numerare* is strange in Latin and is quite probably a translation of the Greek ἄρχω ἀπό σου, which appears twice in Demosthenes (*Philippic III* 22; *On the Crown* 297).[15] Moreover, some of the expression in this section is very Demosthenic. Rapidity is achieved by the suppression of main verbs: "Alii postulare illum . . . Alii remittere eum . . . alii nihil eum iam nisi modeste postulare" (2). The dangling adverb and parenthesis ("—praeclare: ex qua non legiones solum sed etiam nationes ad urbem conetur adducere—") that comment on the preceding thought, especially in a sarcastic way, are also Demosthenic (cf. *Philippic III* 25). The metaphorical language, referring to Antony as a "fax," which relates the opponent to natural elements of destruction in the universe, is also possibly of Demosthenic inspiration.

Thus, in the manner of Demosthenes, Cicero clearly marks off with a proverb of sorts the first part of the section preceding the proposal, that is, the argument that the rumors spread by the supporters of Antony should not be believed. He then passes, without hesitation or transition, but indicating clearly to the audience where he is going, to the next argument in this section, the *popularis* theme. This theme is related to and a subtle variation on what precedes, although Cicero, like Demosthenes, does not say at the outset exactly how it is related ("points successifs plutôt qu'enchaînés"): "Atque haec ei loquuntur qui quondam propter levitatem populares habebantur" (4). Cicero is doing something in this passage that Demosthenes does quite often, redefining political terms in an attempt to broaden his base of support as much as possible. Both Cicero, at this time, and Demosthenes, when he began to be concerned about the problems of northern Greece, were associated with the conservative, less democratically oriented elements in the state; however, they both realized that in order to defeat the enemy they must turn to all segments of the state for support. Demosthenes therefore turned to the people[16] and on several occasions attempted to redefine the term δημοτικός.[17] Cicero, likewise, in this speech continues to isolate himself from his opponents by making a distinction between "popularis," which they claim to be, and "voluntate popularis," those who are truly concerned about the welfare of the state. Thus, like Demosthenes (cf. *On the Crown* 122), Cicero defines the term in a more general way and more elevated sense, to make the contrast between himself and his opponents clearer: "Il veut ainsi opposer à la tradition démocratique de son temps, qui est parfaitement inconsistante et n'apporte rien au peuple, une nouvelle conception du 'popularis,' qui s'appuie sur une véritable programme politique ou qui, tout au moins, peut à cette époque prétendre à ce titre. . . . il était temps de s'élever, il le voyait bien, à une conception plus 'universelle' de la politique, de chercher, non le profit d'une classe, mais le bien de toute la population."[18] Thus, in reviving his conception of the *concordia ordinum*, Cicero, like Demosthenes, becomes the teacher of his people.[19]

The passage subtly develops one aspect of the argument that precedes, the real difference between Cicero and Antony's supporters, although Cicero sees himself merely as the representative of the loyal elements in the state. He continues this argument, again with no transition, in section 5 by picking up and elaborating another element of it, the theme that Antony's supporters are undermining the state and the implication that they are in Antony's pay; again the tactic that he uses is a definition of political terms: "Et quidem dicuntur vel potius se ipsi dicunt consularis" (5). These men, Cicero argues, who openly support the enemy cannot be considered true consulars:

> Faveas tu hosti? ille litteras ad te mittat de sua spe rerum secundarum; eas tu laetus proferas, recites, describendas etiam des improbis civibus, eorum augeas animos, bonorum spem virtutemque debilites, et te consularem aut senatorem, denique civem putes?" (5)

The last phrase, reminiscent of section 12 of *Philippic IV*, where he describes Antony in the same terms, shows clearly that Cicero considers these men in the same way.

This is quite similar to the utter contempt that one finds over and over again in Demosthenes for the openness with which people betray the state and the conviction that they are the ones who are the real cause of Athens' problems:

> What is the situation? Envy, if anyone has taken a bribe. Laughter, if he admits it. Pardon to those who are convicted. Hatred, if anyone reproaches such practices. . . . all our resources are rendered useless, impracticable, worthless by these traitors. (*Philippic III* 39–40)

So, one sees how Cicero, like Demosthenes, takes an idea and then, moving in an orderly manner, with no appearance of hesitation and no transitions, making one point at a time, subtly elaborates and develops that idea from various points of view. Here the discussion of what a "popularis" is and of how a "consularis" should act elaborates the attack on Antony's agents that he develops in sections 2 and 3 by looking at them in various ways and undercutting their credibility. Although there is no attempt to state explicitly what the relationship between these fairly discrete units is, that relationship is quite obvious: "The most obvious Demosthenic parallel in this part of the speech is the technique which places opposing arguments in the mouths of people who are later shown to be ignorant and at worst, co-conspirators of the enemy."[20] Moreover, the lack of transition adds to the directness and speed of the argumentation and creates something that certainly approaches "la rapide simplicité de Démosthènes."

Cicero continues to elaborate this attack on his opponents in the next passage, which he addresses to the consul Pansa, by showing the obverse of Antony's agents, just as Demosthenes, especially in the speech *On the Crown*, consistently pairs the positive with the negative, emphasizing what a true statesman should be by comparing him with what a true statesman is not.[21] He says of Pansa: "Nisi talis consul esset ut omnis vigilias, curas, cogitationes in rei publicae salute defigeret, consulem non putarem" (5). This leads to the argument that Pansa is the greatest of all consuls, a seeming paradox that thus attracts the attention of the audience. Demosthenes often uses paradoxes in this way (cf. *Philippic III* 5). Cicero soon explains himself, however, by pointing out that Pansa is consul during the greatest crisis in Roman history: "Alii . . . tantam causam non habuerunt in qua et voluntatem suam et virtutem declarent" (6). He closes this first section of the speech by returning in ring composition to the motif with which it began (cf. sec. 1), the crisis that threatens the state: "Magis autem necessarium, patres conscripti, nul-

lum tempus umquam fuit" (7). Moreover, he indicates clo-
sure of this section by the use of an image that is surely of
Demosthenic origin: Pansa is the helmsman (the "guber-
nator") who will guide the state through the storm of crisis
("tempestas formidolosissimi temporis").[22]

   Like Demosthenes, Cicero has prepared his audience to
receive favorably his point of view by a preliminary argument, here a nicely nuanced attack on his opponents, the
supporters of Antony. Having brought this section to a
close with an image and a restatement of the theme with
which he opened the speech, as Demosthenes often does
(cf. *Philippic I* 2, 13), he then embarks upon a long and
disjointed, even tortuous, sentence (7–8), filled with parentheses and qualifiers, that leads up to and thus high-
lights the point he wants to make, which, by contrast, is
stated very simply at the end: "pacem cum M. Antonio
esse nolo" (8). This sentence has perplexed commentators, who refer to it as being "unbalanced" and "spastic."[23]
In Demosthenic terms, however, it is quite explicable.
Demosthenes is fond of using long and involved sentences,
filled with apologies and qualifiers, to build up to a conclusion, which is curtly and emphatically, even joltingly, set
off from the rest of the sentence at the end. This procedure, like the use of paradox, calls attention to an important point by arousing the audience's interest and then
by contrasting rather abruptly the simple, if unexpected,
conclusion with what precedes. The first sentence of the
Third Philippic is a good example:

> Although, men of Athens, there are many speeches
> at almost every meeting of the assembly concerning
> the wrongs that Philip has done, not only to you, but
> also to the others, from the time when he made the
> peace, and although all would agree, even if they do
> not do this, that it is necessary both to speak and to
> act in such a way as to put an end to his arrogance
> and to punish him for it, I see that all our interests
> have been neglected to such an extent that—I fear

that it is a bad omen to say it but that it is true—
even if all the politicians had wanted to propose and
you had been willing to enact measures by which
the situation would be as bad as possible, I do not
think that it could be worse than it is now. (1)

Demosthenes uses the same sort of procedure in the
speech *On the Crown*:

But since he emphasizes results so much, I want to
formulate a certain paradox. And, by Zeus and all
the gods, let no one be amazed at my extravagance,
but let him consider what I say with goodwill. For if
the future had been clear to all, and all knew it be-
forehand, and you, Aeschines, had predicted it, and
proved it, shouting and screaming, you, who never
uttered a word, not even then should the city have
abandoned this policy, if it had any consideration for
its reputation or its ancestors or the future. (199)

This is exactly what Cicero is trying to do in the *Seventh Philippic*. He introduces a bold and possibly disturb-
ing thought by setting it off with a long preliminary apology. He says, in fact, after stating his opinion:

Magna spe ingredior in reliquam orationem, patres
conscripti, quoniam periculosissimum locum silen-
tio sum praetervectus. (8)

In addition, he uses Demosthenic motifs to introduce his
conclusion, especially the plea that the audience hear him
out regardless of how strange his argument might sound
because he is speaking only out of concern for the welfare
of the state:

—ego igitur pacis, ut ita dicam, alumnus qui quan-
tuscumque sum (nihil enim mihi adrogo) sine pace
civili certe non fuissem (periculose dico: quem ad
modum accepturi, patres conscripti, sitis, horreo,
sed pro mea perpetua cupiditate vestrae dignitatis

> retinendae et augendae quaeso oroque vos, patres
> conscripti, ut primo, etsi erit vel acerbum auditu vel
> incredibile a M. Cicerone esse dictum, accipiatis
> sine offensione quod dixero, neve id prius quam
> quale sit explicaro repudietis]— (8)

Likewise, in the sentence that concludes this section, he
asks again for the goodwill of his audience:

> Peto a vobis, patres conscripti, ut eadem benignitate
> qua soletis mea verba audiatis. (9)

This sounds very much like the beginning of Demosthenes' speech *On the Crown*, and the "benignitas" that Cicero demands from his audience is surely the εὔνοια that
Demosthenes claims from the Athenians.

In any case, this is exactly the sort of preliminary argument that Demosthenes uses so often (cf. *On the Crown*
5–7; *Philippic III* 3–6). Moreover, the Latin sentence
seems more awkward because of the basic differences between Greek and Latin. In the passage quoted earlier from
the *Third Philippic*, for example, Demosthenes can keep
the sentence from becoming too disjointed by the use of
participles and genitive absolutes, which allow him to
combine many thoughts fairly smoothly into a whole.
Cicero, on the other hand, has to resort more to bulky
clauses and parentheses because he writes in Latin. The
basic intention of the approach, however, is Demosthenic.

Also Demosthenic is the procedure of leading into the
argumentation with a rhetorical question, especially after
a paradoxical statement. In the *First Philippic*, for example, Demosthenes says:

> For what is worst from the past is best in reference
> to the future. What then is this? (2)

Likewise, after this long and involved sentence, Cicero
moves to an unexpected conclusion:

> Cur igitur pacem nolo? (9)

Moreover, like Demosthenes, he makes it clear at the out-set what his procedure in the argumentation will be:

> Quia turpis est, quia periculosa, quia esse non potest. (9)

As Hermogenes points out (*On Ideas*, Rabe, 235 – 37), it is typical of Demosthenes to make clear to his audience what his procedure will be; and this, as much as anything, contributes to the clarity of his speeches:

> And it is just perhaps that I, having made this prom-ise show you these things, first that the decree is contrary to the laws, second that it is not beneficial to the city, and third that Charidemus is not worthy of it. (*Against Aristocrates* 18)

Hermogenes shows that it is also typical of Demosthenes to give résumés of what has already been argued as a means of transition to the next point:

> On the assumption that you will know and have been persuaded that you must all be ready and will-ing to do what is necessary, I say nothing more. I shall now attempt to say what the nature of the force should be. (*Philippic I* 13).

Cicero does the same thing in this speech. At each point in the argument, he stops, gives a résumé of the point he has already made, and indicates where he is proceeding:

> Satis multa de turpitudine. Dicam deinceps, ut pro-posui, de periculo: quod etsi minus est fugiendum quam turpitudo (16). . . . Dixi de periculo: docebo ne coagmentari quidem posse pacem; de tribus enim quae proposui hoc extremum est. (21)[24]

Unlike many of Cicero's earlier speeches, this speech keeps to the point. There are very few of the digressions and circumlocutions that are often associated with Cice-ronian oratory. He states his argument and then immediately sets out to demonstrate it. In many ways, this regular, tightly organized, and clear-cut development, which dominates the second half of the speech, is its most Demosthenic characteristic, for it makes possible the directness, the speed, the sureness of argumentation that one usually finds in his speeches.[25]

It is not only the structure of the argumentation, however, that is Demosthenic; the arguments themselves are surely of Demosthenic inspiration. George Kennedy has pointed out that in Demosthenes' mature speeches, especially in the *Third Philippic*, all arguments are made subordinate to the necessity to preserve Athenian national character: "Expediency and justice in the old sense are not discussed, yet the whole speech is concerned with the necessity of action in Athens' interest. Failure to act will inevitably bring disgrace for all that Athens has been."[26] Likewise, in this speech Cicero's primary argument, the one that he puts first ("periculo: quod etsi minus est fugiendum quam turpitudo") and that he argues with the most conviction, is that it is disgraceful ("turpis") to make peace with Antony. Moreover, the coupling of arguments from honor, expediency, and possibility that Cicero uses here is quite typical of Demosthenes. In the *Third Olynthiac*, he puts forth an argument typical of those used in the speeches against Philip:

> I see no alternative. For apart from the disgrace that would attach to us if we compromise in any way, I see, men of Athens, quite a lot of danger for the future, if the Thebans are disposed towards us as they are, if the Phocians have been deprived of their resources, and if there is nothing to prevent Philip, when he has control of the present situation, to turn against us. (8)

This is exactly the sort of synthesis of arguments that Cicero uses in the *Seventh Philippic*.

Moreover, not only are the clear structure and the arguments used Demosthenic but the way in which the arguments are developed is also doubtlessly of Demosthenic inspiration. As Demosthenes often does (cf. *Olynthiac I* 11), Cicero opens the argumentation with a general concept:

> Quid est inconstantia, levitate, mobilitate cum singulis hominibus, tum vero universo senatui turpius? (9)

He then relates the particular issue at hand to this general concept:

> Quid porro inconstantius quam quem modo hostem non verbo sed re multis decretis iudicavistis, cum hoc subito pacem velle coniungi? (9–10)

Cicero then gives a résumé of the decrees of the senate, repeating eight times from sections 10 through 14 the idea "Antonius hostis est." Demosthenes is also fond of the procedure of making a point emphatic by repeating it over and over again in reference to different specific examples, which he piles one on top of the other; and he often repeats a phrase to make the parallels clear.[27] Cicero too is careful to vary his repetition and his presentation. He makes a statement about the senate's decrees concerning Octavian and the soldiers who support him, then he deals with the decrees concerning Brutus and the consuls in a series of rhetorical questions, then he makes a brief digression about the health of Hirtius, then he returns to a series of rhetorical questions concerning the people's opposition to Antony.[28] In the repetition of the leitmotiv there is also an effort at variety, reflecting the variety of the groups that have condemned Antony:

> Hostem tum Antonium iudicavistis. . . . hostis est a vobis iudicatus Antonius. . . . tum hostem Antonium iudicastis. . . . cum esset hostis. . . . tum non hostem iudicastis Antonium? . . . si hostis Antonius

> non erat? . . . tum ille hostis non est iudicatus? . . .
> non est iudicatus hostis Antonius? (10–14)

Cicero's presentation, however, is usually more emphatic than Demosthenes' use of similar techniques.[29] However, his ability to focus attention on a single point and to bring it out from many points of view contributes even more than variety to the Demosthenic quality of this section of the speech. As Delaunois says, in speaking of another speech against Antony: "Cicéron frappe avec énergie dès le début, lui aussi sait 'canonner' comme Démosthène."[30]

After this "proof" that Antony is a "hostis," Cicero then has an imaginary interlocutor make an objection that allows him to continue to develop his argument, as Demosthenes does so frequently:

> "At legatos misimus." Heu, me miserum! cur senatum cogor, quem laudavi semper, reprehendere? (14)

This allows him to repeat in summary form the arguments used in an earlier speech, here the *Fifth Philippic*, against sending an embassy to Antony; and Demosthenes often uses such a technique in his speeches against Philip. Cicero's recapitulation of arguments then leads up to a moving section, very much in the spirit of the end of Demosthenes' *Third Philippic*, that is written in the simple and direct style of much of Cicero's speeches against Antony:

> Liberati regio dominatu videbamur: multo postea gravius urgebamur armis domesticis. Ea ipsa depulimus nos quidem: extorquenda sunt. Quod si non possumus facere—dicam quod dignum est et senatore et Romano homine—moriamur. (14)

This is very characteristic of Demosthenes and very similar to the sort of emotional outbursts to which he often builds up in his speeches:

> And yet may the situation, men of Athens, not
> reach that point. But it is better to die a thousand
> times than to do anything out of flattery to Philip.
> (*Philippic III* 65).

Cicero concludes this section with a narration of Antony's crimes and the only conclusion that one can reach
when he contemplates those actions: "Ob has ipsas cau-
sas hostis iudicatus est" (15).

What is really most Demosthenic about this whole section is Cicero's ability to focus his attention on a single
and simple thought, namely, that Antony is an enemy of
the state and that it is shameful to deal with such a man.
He brings out that argument from several points of view,
using decrees of the senate, moral abstractions, narration
of events, emotion, logic, and moral sensitivity to reinforce one basic proposition. It is this sort of argumentation that conveys to the audience the certainty and clarity
with which the orator views the situation and compels
them to look at it in the same way.

The other two arguments are developed similarly. In the
discussion of the perilous nature of the situation, Cicero
returns to an attack on Antony's brother Lucius, very
similar to the one in the *Sixth Philippic* (10–15). What
Cicero stresses here is that Lucius, the mirror image of
his brother, is the worst enemy of those groups in the
state that he claims to represent (16–17), and to bring this
out he uses the same sort of ironic contrast favored by Demosthenes. Cicero constructs a series of sentences whose
parallelism underlines his argument:

> Est enim patronus quinque et triginta tribuum,
> quarum sua lege . . . suffragium sustulit; patronus
> centuriarum equitum Romanorum quas item sine
> suffragio esse voluit, patronus eorum qui tribuni
> militares fuerunt, patronus Iani medii. Quis huius
> potentiam poterit sustinere? (16)

Demosthenes also uses this sort of contrast between ironic statement and reality, and, as Cicero does here, he avoids the monotony of overly strict parallelism while retaining the effect of basically repeating a pattern:[31]

> The people of Oreus have received a noble reward for entrusting themselves to the friends of Philip and driving out Euphraeus. The people of Eretria have received a noble reward for driving out your ambassadors and entrusting themselves to Clitarchus. They are slaves now who are whipped and butchered. Nobly did he spare the Olynthians who chose Lasthenes hipparch and drove out Apollonides. (*Philippic III* 65–66)

Then, in an attempt to generalize his attack, Cicero relates the "Antonios" to other revolutionaries who have threatened Rome, just as Demosthenes consistently compares Philip's threats against Greece to other occasions on which the Athenians have been the champions of Greek liberty: "Gracchorum potentiam maiorem fuisse arbitramini quam huius gladiatoris futura sit?" (17). There follows a discussion of Lucius's cruelty that is related to his activities as a gladiator,[32] especially the episode in Asia when he butchered one of his friends for sport. Using an argument a fortiori, which sounds very much like an argument that Demosthenes uses in reference to Philip, Cicero asks his audience to try to imagine how a man who treats friends thus, when all that is at stake is sport, would treat his enemies, when what is at stake is great gain:

> Qui familiarem iugularit, quid is occasione data faciet inimico? et qui illud animi causa fecerit, hunc praedae causa quid facturum putastis? (18)

Demosthenes makes the same point about Philip:

> Has he not deprived the Thebans of Echinus, and is he not now marching against the Byzantines, al-

though they are his allies? . . . And yet what do you
think that one who treats us all so brutally will do
when he has become the master of us one by one?
(*Philippic III* 34−35)

Cicero then makes it clear, by an abrupt transition, that
Lucius is only an image of his brother ("M. vero Antonius
non is erit ad quem"), who is the real object of attack,[33]
and that the greatest source of danger is the barbarity and
cruelty of the opponent and of the evil men who have
flocked to him. Demosthenes makes the same point
about Philip: Philip will spare no one who is in the way of
his ambition (*Philippic III* 57−62), and he is surrounded
by evil men who spur him on (*Olynthiac II* 18−19). This
is the greatest source of danger facing the state.

   Cicero concludes this section with several Demosthenic commonplaces. One of these, at least, is so obvious that we can almost imagine Cicero with the text of
Demosthenes before him; and this again is surely an attempt on Cicero's part to call attention to his indebted-
ness to Demosthenes.[34] There is first the *kairos* theme developed earlier:

   Ego vero metuo, si hoc tempore consilio lapsi
   erimus, ne illi brevi tempore nimis multi nobis
   esse videantur. (18)

Second, Cicero does not fear peace but war that is called
peace; and if the senate wants a lasting peace, it must
wage war now:

   Nec ego pacem nolo, sed pacis nomine bellum invo-
   lutum reformido. Qua re si pace frui volumus,
   bellum gerendum est; si bellum omittimus, pace
   numquam fruemur. (19)

Demosthenes argues in the *Third Philippic* exactly the
same point that we see in the first sentence of the passage
quoted above:

> But if someone else, with arms in his hands and
> great power, offers to you the *name* of peace, but en-
> gages in the acts of war, what can we do except de-
> fend ourselves? And if you want to *say* that you are
> at peace, as he does, I do not object. But if anyone
> supposes this situation to be peace . . . he is
> mad. (8–9)[35]

Likewise, Demosthenes often uses the argument that,
ironically, only war now can bring a lasting peace. In the
Olynthiacs he repeatedly makes the point that the only
way to prevent an invasion of Attica is to fight Philip in
the north:

> By the gods, who of you is so foolish who does not
> know that the war there will come here if we are
> negligent? (*Olynthiac I* 15)

In the third of the Demosthenic commonplaces concluding this argument, Cicero maintains that it is the role of
the politician to foresee the future (cf. *Philippic I* 50); like
Demosthenes (cf. *Philippic I* 39), he compares the senate
to a soldier posted at his station. Then, again like Demosthenes, he calls attention to the clarity of the situation
("in re tam perspicua"), outlines the resources of the state
that give reason to be hopeful, and pledges his vigilance
and energy for the state (cf. *On the Chersonese* 75–77).

The third section of argumentation, like the first two,
shows again Cicero's skill with the basically Demosthenic technique of taking the simple facts of the case and
nuancing them in such a way as to prove another point. In
other words, he uses the same facts to demonstrate quite
a different argument.[36] Cicero argues here that the decrees
of the senate, the actions of Antony, the attitude of the
Roman people, the activities of the Italians, all of which
he has discussed before, make it impossible for the state
to conclude a peace with Antony.[37] The views represented
by the senate, on the one hand, and Antony, on the other,
are, Cicero argues, mutually exclusive; and this brings

out again the disjunctive nature of the argument in these speeches. There can be only hatred between Antony and the forces that the senate represents:

> Quis vestrum illum, quem ille vestrum non *oderit*?
> . . . *amici* umquam vobis erunt aut vos illis? . . . hi
> Antonium *diligent*? (21)

Demosthenes also frequently uses this argument concerning the mutual hatred that must exist between those who love liberty and those who represent slavery:

> "What do you seek?" I said. "Freedom. Then do you
> not see that Philip even has titles that are inimical
> to this? For every king and despot is the enemy of
> freedom and the opponent of laws." (*Philippic II* 25)

It is interesting, moreover, that after discussing the various opponents of Antony in general terms, Cicero then deals with the actions of a specific individual:

> Ut omittam multitudinem, L. Visidio . . . poteritne
> esse pacatus Antonius? (24)

This seems a rather strange procedure, to single out an individual as a representative of a general attitude, until one remembers the effectiveness with which Demosthenes so often supports a general thesis by singling out a specific example (e.g., Arthmius of Zelea and Euphraeus in *Philippic III* 41–46, 59–62), which is often more compelling than a general discussion.[38] Cicero then concludes this section with a repetition of the idea that concluded the previous one: "Nolite igitur id velle quod fieri non potest, et cavete, per deos immortalis! patres conscripti, ne spe praesentis pacis perpetuam pacem amittatis" (25).

The third section of argumentation, like the first two, is well organized. In giving his examples of the various groups in the state who hate Antony, Cicero deals, in order, with the senate, the knights, the whole Roman people, the boroughs of Italy, the Marrucinians, Lucius Visidius, Octavian, and Brutus, thus expanding his catalog and then becoming more specific again, moving smoothly from the specific to the general and then back to the specific. This tightly knit organization, as has been seen, is typical of the entire speech.[39]

Cicero concludes the speech with a restatement, again in the simplest terms, of what is at stake here: "Libertas agitur populi Romani" (27). He also uses an apt image of Antony as a wild beast that has been shut up momentarily but should not be let out, again underlining the basic conflict in these speeches between the opposing forces of liberty and slavery, reason and passion, order and uncontrolled violence: "Taetram et pestiferam beluam ne inclusam et constrictam demittatis cavete" (27).

Finally one general feature of this speech, and of all the *Philippics* with the exception of the *Second*, that contributes to its directness and that conveys the certainty of the speaker and the clarity with which he views the situation is the relative absence of Cicero himself from the speech. Unlike his earlier speeches, there is very little in this speech about the speaker. Gone are the rambling digressions about Cicero's views on philosophy and government and his attempts to justify or qualify his own position. As Pearson says of Demosthenes' mature speeches: "There are a few 'ego's' still in the speech *On the Liberty of the Rhodians*, but in the *First Philippic* the personal pronoun appears only in enclitic form, and when he uses the first person singular form of a verb, it is without an 'ego,' except in the closing paragraphs where he is summing up and tendering his personal conclusions."[40] Cicero's ability to concentrate on the situation and on what must be done to solve it, to present his arguments objectively even at the expense of a certain amount of ethical appeal, and to deal with the situation directly contributes a great deal to the "cleanness" of the *Seventh Philippic* and creates "an intensity and a fervor all too typical of Demosthenes' *Philippics*."[41]

Chapter 6

Style and Narrative Technique:

Philippics VIII, IX, X, and *XI*

The *Eighth Philippic* was delivered on 3 February 43 B.C., after the return of the unsuccessful embassy to Antony, on which one of the ambassadors, Servius Sulpicius Rufus, had died. Like the *Seventh Philippic*, this speech is well organized. Here, however, Cicero is less explicit about the organizational structure that he will follow and is thus really more like Demosthenes in this respect.[1] After a preliminary rebuke to those members of the senate who had opposed him on the preceding day, the speech falls into three clearly defined sections: the nature of the conflict against Antony (2–10); a criticism of the ambassadors who yielded to Antony and of Antony himself, coupled with a defense of Cicero's own position (23–33); and a concluding formal proposal.

Within each of these three major sections, the argumentation once again is clearly developed, and Cicero moves without hesitation from one point to the next. This is especially true in the first section that deals with the nature of the conflict against Antony and is an answer to those who, on the preceding day, had objected to the use of the word *bellum* in the senate's decree. In this section Cicero looks at the issue from several points of view, concluding in each case that the conflict with Antony is a *bellum* and repeating in each section of the argumentation certain basic themes that hold this entire part of the speech together.

Cicero's first argument is based on semantics, that the term *tumultus*, which his opponents want to use, necessarily implies the existence of a *bellum* because a *tumultus* historically had always referred to a particular kind of *bellum* or to one aspect of a more general war, that is, fighting in or near Italy: "Potest enim esse bellum ut tumultus non sit, tumultus autem esse sine bello non potest" (2). As is only appropriate, this section is written in the clear, full, and lucid expository style that one usually associates with Cicero's philosophical works, the style that Hermogenes calls amplification or abundance:

> Etenim cum inter bellum et pacem medium nihil sit, necesse est tumultum, si belli non sit, pacis esse: quo quid absurdius dici aut existimari potest? (4)

The argument, based on etymology, example, comparison, and syllogistic reasoning, and the style, in which every point in the argument is fully, often even redundantly, explained, both give this section a cool, logical tone, the same sort of style that Demosthenes often uses when he is explaining a term:

> Let no man be acquitted nor anyone condemned merely because this man or that one desires it, but whomever the facts acquit or condemn, let him receive from you the verdict that he deserves, for this is the democratic spirit. (*On the False Embassy* 296).

Then, also like Demosthenes (cf. *Philippic I* 13), Cicero clearly indicates the termination of this argument, based on "verba," and shows that he will pass to an argument based on "res": "Sed nimis multa de verbo: rem potius videamus" (4). He also indicates at the outset what is at issue in this section of the speech: "Nolumus hoc bellum videri." Here, moreover, we see Cicero's ability to switch rapidly to the plain style, what Hermogenes calls clarity, when his only intention is to state a simple fact, as Demosthenes often does to indicate the point at stake in a section of argumentation:

> The present crisis, more than ever, demands great thought and consideration. (*Olynthiac III* 3)
> It is necessary that our expedition be large and two-fold. (*Olynthiac I* 18)

The tone, however, of the second step in the argumentation changes swiftly from the logical exposition of the preceding section to the more heated tone of debate. Cicero argues in three fairly short rhetorical questions, introduced by the impatient interrogative "quam," that unless there is a war the senate has no authority to coordinate actions all over Italy against Antony (4), arguing from effect to cause. These questions are purely rhetorical (*erōtēmata*), the most emotional type of question, asked not to obtain information or to introduce an argument but simply to express amazement and anger.[2] He then reverts to the logical tone of exposition, similar to that of the preceding section, to explain the effect that the failure to use the term *bellum* would have on the loyal supporters of the senate:

> Si enim belli nomen tolletur, municipiorum studia tollentur; consensus populi Romani, qui iam descendit in causam, si nos languescimus, debilitetur necesse est. (4)

He returns immediately, however, to the more emotional tone of the rhetorical questions, which is intensified by sarcasm and irony. This is the style Hermogenes calls asperity, to be used when the orator reproaches some group more important than himself:

> D. Brutus oppugnatur: non est bellum? Mutina obsidetur: ne hoc quidem bellum est? Gallia vastatur: quae pax potest esse certior? (5)

The repetition of the pattern consisting of a very straightforward and obvious statement of fact followed by a question as to how it should interpreted, coupled with the repetition of basically the same question after each statement, with typically Demosthenic variety, underlines the irony of the situation. How, Cicero asks sarcastically, could anyone interpret such simple facts to be anything other than war? The climax also brings out the absurdity of the question: As Antony attacks a man, then a city, then a whole province, the question following the statement becomes longer and the contrast between fact and interpretation more obvious.

Then, after a series of five sarcastic questions, Cicero constructs two periodic sentences to describe two unified actions against Antony, one by the senate and the consul and the other by Octavian. In these sentences, moreover, one sees the Demosthenic or analytical period, with the main thought at the outset, which Cicero prefers in these speeches:

> Consulem . . . misimus, qui, cum esset . . . C. quidem Caesar non exspectavit vestra decreta, praesertim cum . . . (5)

After this calm narration of unified events, in a style that Hermogenes would call beauty, Cicero reverts to the sarcastic tone of the preceding rhetorical questions. His ironic comment on the actions of Hirtius and Octavian against Antony is:

> Ergo illi nunc et eorum exercitus in pace
> versantur. (6)

He continues this ironical pattern of the juxtaposition of an interpretation, here the wrong one rather than one that is in doubt, and an obvious fact:

> Non est hostis is cuius . . . non est hostis qui. . . . (6)

Here, moreover, one sees again typically Demosthenic variety in the presentation of a pattern. The first relative clause, introduced by "cuius," is short; the second, introduced by "qui," is long, consisting of three separate clauses that outline Antony's actions against the state and conclude with a quotation from Hirtius's letter to the senate. Also, the third element in the pattern is totally different in structure, although the basic point is the same:

> Quae pax potest esse maior? Dilectus tota Italia decreti sublatis vacationibus; saga cras sumentur; consul se cum praesidio descensurum esse dixit. (6)

One sees, therefore, in these two sections, as in the whole speech, the typically Demosthenic ability to vary tone and style; the mixture of statement, sarcastic outburst, narration, and argumentation; and the sense of propriety that knows how to vary style to suit the tone and intent of the individual passage and to show restraint in the use of figures, in the construction of periods, and in the enumeration of examples. It is surely the variety and restraint of this speech that is most Demosthenic. Throughout this section, to prove the point that the conflict with Antony is a *bellum*, Cicero is basically juxtaposing facts and how those facts should be interpreted; however, he varies the presentation of the pattern considerably, using short statements followed by questions, long periods followed by ironic comment, ironic statements in which the main clause is contrasted with the relative clause, and ironic questions followed by straightforward responses.

Cicero then indicates clearly the next topic that he will treat, thus giving the speech distinctness, which Hermogenes repeatedly points out as being so characteristic of the speeches of Demosthenes. He passes without hesitation to the comparison of this war with other civil wars and the argument that this is more serious than all of them: "Utrum hoc bellum non est, an est tantum bellum quantum numquam fuit?" (7). As a means of transition, he here uses, as Demosthenes often does,[3] an *aetiologia*, a question that the orator asks himself and to which he then provides the answer. Cicero returns here to the calm tone of exposition that we saw earlier. He first states a premise: "Ceteris enim bellis maximeque civilibus contentionem rei publicae causa faciebat" (7). Then he supports this premise with three historical examples that are stated as simply as possible, as is appropriate to the narration of historical facts, and that follow a regular order to underline the fact that they all illustrate the same point: "Sulla cum Sulpicio . . . ; Cinna cum Octavio . . . ; rursus cum Mario et Carbone Sulla" (7). There is variety, however. In each case, the verb is omitted; but in the first the cause is given in a prepositional phrase followed by a relative clause, in the second by a simple prepositional phrase, and in the third by two purpose clauses, one negative and one positive. Then the premise is restated: "Horum omnium bellorum causae ex rei publicae contentione natae sunt" (7). This pattern—premise, examples to prove it, restatement of premise—is one of which Demosthenes is also fond (cf. *Philippic III* 10–14), although Cicero's presentation is usually briefer and developed with more clarity than is common in Demosthenes.[4]

Then, after a fleeting comment about the civil war between Pompey and Caesar, Cicero comes to the point of this historical digression, the thesis that this civil war is different from the others. Consequently, he reverts to the full and repetitive style appropriate to logical exposition, what Hermogenes calls the abundant style so typical of Demosthenes:

> Hoc bellum quintum civile geritur—atque omnia in nostram aetatem inciderunt—primum non modo non in dissensione et discordia civium sed in maxima consensione incredibilique concordia. Omnes idem volunt, idem defendunt, idem sentiunt. (8)

It is interesting that here Cicero, like Demosthenes, not only uses repetition to make his thought clear but also sums up the thought of a fairly long sentence in a short and more direct sentence that follows it; and the anaphora and parallelism in this sentence may reflect the harmony in Italy that Cicero wants to convey.

He then introduces the next segment of the argument, again without hesitation or transition, as he and Demosthenes often do (cf. *Philippic I* 47), with a rhetorical question, once more an *aetiologia*: "Quae est igitur in medio belli causa posita?" Here Cicero lapses again into the disjunctive mode, and to bring out clearly the difference between loyal Romans and Antony he uses a more extreme form of parallelism and antithesis than one usually finds in these speeches, although there is still quite a lot of variety:

> Nos deorum immortalium templa, nos muros, nos domicilia sedesque populi Romani, aras, focos, sepulcra maiorum; nos leges, iudicia, libertatem, coniuges, liberos, patriam defendimus: contra M. Antonius id molitur, id pugnat ut haec omnia perturbet, evertat, praedam rei publicae causam belli putet, fortunas nostras partim dissipet partim dispertiat parricidis. (8)

It is not only the structure that underlines the difference between loyal Romans and Antony. The first section is filled with nouns, reflecting the stability that Cicero and his supporters defend; the second section is filled with verbs, mainly those that reflect disorder, as can be seen in the repeated prefix "dis." It is striking, however, how carefully Cicero has avoided exact parallelism in a sentence where it would appear fairly natural.

Cicero continues the contrast in the next section (9–10), in which he discusses the difference between what Antony can offer his supporters and what the senate can offer its own. Once again, it is remarkable that Cicero, except in the very last sentence of the section, avoids the strict parallelism and antithesis that one might expect here. Like Demosthenes, he prefers antithesis of thought

to strict antithesis in structure because he must have
come to realize that "the constant juxtaposing of two
opposite ideas becomes trite and monotonous with its
metronome-like regularity."[5] In three sentences with the
basically simple structure of subject-verb, modified by a
few simple subordinate clauses, he describes what Antony promises his supporters and what they expect for
themselves (9). Such a style is appropriate to what purports, at least, to be the simple narration of facts. The
clear transition would lead one to expect a parallel structure following the transitional phrase:

> Ergo habet Antonius quod suis polliceatur. Quid
> nos? num quid tale habemus? Di meliora! (9)

However, the response is quite different and unexpected:

> Id enim ipsum agimus ne quis posthac quicquam
> eius modi possit polliceri. (9)

There is then a rather abrupt digression on the effect that
Caesar's conscriptions had on many Romans, underlining
again the chaos that Caesar and his successor Antony
have created in Rome: "Viderunt enim ex mendicis fieri
repente divites" (9). This may be modeled on a similar
phrase in Demosthenes (cf. *On the Chersonese* 66 and
Against Aristocrates 209). Then he returns to his previous question:

> Quid? Nos nostris exercitibus quid pollicemur?
> Multo meliora atque maiora. (10)

The two clauses of the first sentence of Cicero's reply are
strictly parallel neither in thought nor in structure. In the
second, however, he finally expresses the sort of strict parallelism and antithesis that one has been expecting:

> Scelerum enim promissio et eis qui exspectant per-
> niciosa est et eis qui promittunt: nos libertatem
> nostris militibus, leges, iura, iudicia, imperium orbis
> terrae, dignitatem, pacem, otium pollicemur. Antoni

igitur promissa cruenta, taetra, scelerata, dis homi-
nibusque invisa, nec diuturna neque salutaria:
nostra contra honesta, integra, gloriosa, plena
laetitiae, plena pietatis. (10)

In other words, Cicero has clearly set up the expectation
of a strict antithesis and then, at least until the end of the
passage, has foiled that expectation, as Demosthenes often does, through the use of inconcinnity or purposeful
avoidance of symmetry and balance. Such strategy is unusual in Cicero, but it avoids the appearance of artificiality. Strict parallelism and antithesis, like the periodic
structure, is reserved for creating a very special effect at
an emphatic point of the argument.

The reply to Q. Fufius Calenus (11–20), the next major
section of the speech, is most striking in its use of the
simple style of direct statement, the style that Hermogenes calls clarity, which is so typical of Demosthenes.
This style, which one sees more frequently in all the *Philippics* than in Cicero's earlier speeches, is overwhelm-
ingly predominant here. Simple sentences follow one another in rapid sucession, usually with no adornment, no
subordination, no elaboration, and often no transition. In
fact, probably the best description of this section is Galen
Rowe's comment on Demosthenes' *On the Crown*: "The
most common expressive structure in the oration is the
simple clause, by which is meant the presentation of a
complete thought with little or no subordination."[6] The
rapidity and clarity of this style can be seen very well in
the following passage in which Cicero criticizes Fufius's
support of Antony. As Demosthenes often does, he opens
the attack with a type of rhetorical question known as a
hypophora,[7] in which he asks the adversary his opinion
and then immediately counters with his own refutation:

Quo usque enim dices pacem velle te? Res geritur;
conductae vineae sunt; pugnatur acerrime. Qui in-
tercurrerent, misimus tris principes civitatis. Hos

> contempsit, reiecit, repudiavit Antonius: tu tamen
> permanes constantissimus defensor Antonii. (17)

The simple language and the simple structure, usually consisting of subject-verb-object, give to this passage the vivid clarity that one often associates with Lysias. However, this passage contains another virtue that one usually associates with Demosthenes; and that is force. The synonymity in the second and fourth sentences and the abrupt contrasts throughout the passage give the description the same sort of powerful and moving quality that Demosthenes added to the Lysianic style.[8] In this passage, as one critic has written of Demosthenes, Cicero is like "the artist who with a few strokes of charcoal can capture and bring to life all the essential details" of a situation.[9]

One sees elsewhere in this section the economy with which Cicero, like Demosthenes, can vividly present his point of view, using a style that Hermogenes calls rapidity:

> Sed quaeso, Calene, quid tu? Servitutem pacem
> vocas? Maiores quidem nostri non modo ut liberi es-
> sent sed etiam ut imperarent, arma capiebant: tu
> arma abicienda censes ut serviamus? Quae causa
> iustior est belli gerendi quam servitutis depulsio? in
> qua etiam si non sit molestus dominus, tamen est
> miserrimum posse, si velit. Immo aliae causae
> iustae, haec necessaria est. (12)

Here, the basically simple sentences, the short and concise subordinate clauses that usually consist of only two or three words, and the quick, direct movement from one thought to another give the passage a rapidity of proof that is so characteristic of Demosthenes:

> However, all these feelings lie smouldering now,
> since they have no outlet because of your indolence
> and apathy, which I say that you must throw off
> now. For see, gentlemen of Athens, the situation, the
> height of insolence that the man has reached, who

does not give you a choice of action or inaction, but he threatens and talks big, as they say, and he is not able to remain content with what he has subdued, but he is always taking in more, and surrounds us, as we sit and hesitate, on all sides with a net. (*Philippic I* 9–10)

As in the preceding passage from Demosthenes, Cicero uses this direct style, in which bare statement predominates over embellishment or qualification, to pile up examples to prove a point. This style appears in the following passage, in which he justifies military action against Roman citizens on the basis of past traditions:

Quo in proelio Lentulus grave volnus accepit, interfectus est Gracchus et M. Fulvius consularis, eiusque duo adulescentuli filii. Illi igitur viri vituperandi: non enim omnis civis salvos esse voluerunt. Ad propria veniamus. C. Mario L. Valerio consulibus senatus rem publicam defendendam dedit: L. Saturninus tribunus plebis, C. Glaucia praetor est interfectus. Omnes illo die Scauri, Metelli, Claudii, Catuli, Scaevoli, Crassi arma sumpserunt. Num aut consules illos aut clarissimos viros vituperandos putas? Ego Catilinam perire volui. Num tu qui omnis salvos vis Catilinam salvum esse voluisti? Hoc interest, Calene, inter meam sententiam et tuam. Ego nolo quemquam civem committere ut morte multandus sit; tu, etiam si commiserit, conservandum putas. (14–15)

Then, as Demosthenes often does (cf. *Philippic III* 32–34), Cicero uses the momentum of the direct and rapid elements in the catalog to build up to an image, which clearly sums up his thought, and an emotional outburst, which parodies the viewpoint of his opponent:

In corpore si quid eius modi est quod reliquo corpori noceat, id uri secarique patimur ut membrum ali-

> quid potius quam totum corpus intereat. Sic in rei
> publicae corpore, ut totum salvum sit, quicquid est
> pestiferum amputetur. Dura vox! multo illa durior:
> "Salvi sint improbi, scelerati, impii; deleantur inno-
> centes, honesti, boni, tota res publica!" (15–16)

It is interesting, moreover, that Cicero here uses a medical image, a type of which Demosthenes was fond.[10]

One also sees in this section of the speech Cicero's use
of antithesis to sum up his argument and to draw attention to the differences between himself and his opponent.
The most famous instance of this technique in Demosthenes is in the speech *On the Crown*, where Demosthenes compares himself with Aeschines:

> You taught school; I went to school. You initiated
> people; I was initiated. You were a clerk; I was a
> member of the assembly. You were a minor actor; I
> was a spectator. You were hissed; I joined in the
> hissing. You have always served our enemies; I have
> served the fatherland. (262)

Cicero uses the same sort of structure in comparing himself with Calenus, although, as usual, Cicero's development of the idea is briefer than that of Demosthenes:[11]

> Ego huic faveo, tu illi? Immo vero ego D. Bruto
> faveo, tu M. Antonio: ego conservari coloniam po-
> puli Romani cupio, tu expugnari studes. (17)

There are also similarities in development, however. Like
Demosthenes,[12] Cicero, at least in the last contrast, tries
to avoid the danger of excessively parallel, and thus monotonous, development. Moreover, in both passages there
is a progressive development from the less to the more
important.

Cicero clearly signals the transition to the next part of
the argument ("Venio ad reliquos consularis"), as Demosthenes usually does; and here the tone becomes more
emotional. As Cicero himself indicates, the previous sec-

tion was spoken in a subdued manner, "sine iracundia . . . nec tamen sine dolore animi" (19). This section, however, as is often the case in Demosthenes toward the end of the speech (cf. *Philippic III* 65 – 70), shows the impassioned and vehement eloquence that one sees in many of the most famous passages in Demosthenes' speeches.

Provoked by the thought that the ex-consuls on the previous day had supported a second embassy to Antony, Cicero begins this emotional section with an exclamation that reflects a reversal of the light imagery used in earlier speeches (cf. *Philippic V* 2):

Quam hesternus dies nobis . . . *turpis* inluxit! (20)

The two short rhetorical questions that follow also bring out his anger and disbelief. Then, reverting to the simple, direct style, which is again made forceful by synonymity, he relates the cause of his anger:

Ante os oculosque legatorum tormentis Mutinam verberavit; opus ostendebat munitionemque legatis; ne punctum quidem temporis, cum legati adessent, oppugnatio respiravit. (20)

The very thought of the situation provokes more short rhetorical questions (reminiscent of *Philippic V* because they lack verbs) and a sarcastic answer to them, all attempts on Cicero's part to convey his own anger to his audience by using the abrupt language that one often finds in the mouths of angry people:

Ad hunc legatos? cur? an ut eorum reditu vehementius pertimescatis? (20)

One consequently sees here the same sort of mixture of narration and emotional outburst, exclamations and rhetorical questions, that one often finds in Demosthenes (cf. *Philippic II* 15 – 18).

Cicero uses in this section other devices that Demosthenes employs in an attempt to convey his own emotion to his audience. The use of synonymity, contrast, and climax in the following passage, in which Cicero describes what reaction he had expected to the rejected embassy and what he has actually found, is typical of Demosthenes (cf. *On the Crown* 61):

> Ut omnes inflammati odio, excitati dolore, armis, equis, viris D. Bruto subveniremus. Nos etiam languidiores postea facti sumus quam M. Antoni non solum audaciam et scelus sed etiam insolentiam superbiamque perspeximus. (21)

Synonymity and polysyndeton, seen in the second sentence, allow the orator to prolong a thought, to dwell upon it, and thus to impress it more deeply into the minds of his audience.

All of this emotion builds up to the attack that Cicero wants to make on those ex-consuls who support Antony, and his means of expression is pure Demosthenes. To emphasize his point (cf. *On the Crown* 208), he first prepares the audience to receive it by means of a very simple and straightforward sentence:

> Dolenter hoc dicam potius quam contumeliose. (22)

Then he uses epandiplosis and hyperbaton to draw attention to the sentence, which again is stated very directly:

> Deserti, deserti, inquam, sumus, patres conscripti, a principibus. (22)

The abrupt contrast in the description of their actions also emphasizes Cicero's point:

> Animum nobis adferre debuerunt: timorem attulerunt. (22)

The section becomes more emotional again with another exclamation and rhetorical question, appealing, as Demosthenes does so often, to the traditions of the city:

> Pro di immortales! ubi est ille mos virtusque maiorum?" (23)

However, the style switches abruptly, for in a beautifully constructed historical period, exemplary of the extreme control over his language that Cicero shows in the *Philippics*, he gives an example of the "mos virtusque maiorum":

> C. Popilius apud maiores nostros cum ad Antiochum regem legatus missus esset et verbis senatus denuntiasset ut ab Alexandrea discederet quam obsidebat, cum tempus ille differret, virgula stantem circumscripsit dixitque se renuntiaturum senatui, nisi prius sibi respondisset quid facturus esset quam ex illa circumscriptione exisset. (23)

Many elements of this sentence are typically Demosthenic: the control, in which actions that logically preceded the action in the main clause are put before it and those that were logically subsequent to it follow, and the restraint, not only in the brief and straightforward development of the individual clauses, most of which consist of only three or four words and show almost no elaboration of any sort, but also the willingness to use one good example rather than a long series. Too many examples could interrupt the argument like a digression and could be detrimental to the effectiveness of a basically emotional section. The fact that a periodic sentence of this sort is the exception rather than the rule in this speech is also typical of Demosthenes. Demosthenic also is the use of a brief sentence, after this long period, which comments on it and further clarifies the thought:

> Praeclare: senatus enim faciem secum attulerat auctoritatemque rei publicae. (23)

After this brief example, the emotion continues to mount. In fact, the general structure of this speech is very much like that of many of Demosthenes' speeches (cf. *Philippic I*), in which the calm section in the middle is flanked on either side by sections of argument and narration that are more emotional. Here (24) three rhetorical questions and three emotional exclamations describing

Antony's actions lead up to the ironic conclusion, expressed very simply by means of a bold image, as Demosthenes often does (cf. *Philippic I* 40):

> Ferrei sumus, patres conscripti, qui quicquam huic negemus. (25)

Cicero then resorts to another sarcastic procedure of which Demosthenes is also fond, the imaginary dialogue interspersed with the speaker's own commentary (cf. *Philippic I* 10–11). Like the rhetorical questions and exclamations, the dialogue expresses the speaker's anger and bitterness in a form that is intended to evoke the same response in the audience:

> "Utramque provinciam," inquit "remitto: exercitum depono: privatus esse non recuso." Haec sunt enim verba. Redire ad se videtur. "Omnia obliviscor, in gratiam redeo." Sed quid adiungit? "si legionibus meis sex, si equitibus, si cohorti praetoriae praedia agrumque dederitis." (25)

Cicero next comments bitterly on Antony's general demands ("Eis etiam praemia postulat quibus ut ignoscatur si postulet, impudentissimus iudicetur") and constructs most of the rest of this section in a pattern similar to the imaginary dialogue but somewhat changed for the sake of variety. He states one of Antony's demands and then comments on it sarcastically, with a statement or a rhetorical question:

> Addit praeterea. . . . Cavet mimis, aleatoribus, lenonibus. . . . Postulat praeterea. . . . Quid laborat? . . . Postulat enim. . . . Quo impetrato quid est quod metuat? (25–27)

Cicero's reply to each one of Antony's demands is to impute to one or several of his more disreputable adherents ulterior motives that lie behind Antony's conditions. This consistent undercutting of the opposition through ridicule and sarcasm is similar to the discrediting of his opponents in the *Seventh Philippic*. At the end of the passage, he reverts to the imaginary dialogue and ends the attack on Antony with a simple statement bringing out clearly the irony of the situation, a method he prefers in these speeches:

> "Ipse autem ut quinquennium," inquit "obtineam."
> At istud vetat lex Caesaris, et tu acta Caesaris
> defendis. (28)

Then, after ridiculing Antony's demands, he turns in the next major section of the speech to a mild rebuke of the ambassadors who brought back those demands, using the sort of style that Hermogenes calls florescence. This section of the speech is one of the best examples of the rapidity of argumentation that is so characteristic of Cicero's *Philippics*. The passage is composed of several ideas that are logically related, although Cicero moves briskly from one to another without making it perfectly clear what the relationship between them is. As in Demosthenes, there is almost a "stream of consciousness" in which one idea reminds the orator of another to which he moves without hesitation. From mild criticism of the envoys of the senate (28) he moves to a discussion of the difference between the way in which Antony treated the senate's envoys and the way in which the senate has treated Antony's (28). Here he uses a certain amount of parallelism, as is only appropriate; but again, it is parallelism only in thought. The contrast between "vobis . . . clarissimis viris, legatis populi Romani," the qualifier being made even more emphatic by means of hyperbaton, and "legato M. Antoni Cotylae" is indicative of the absurdity of the situation:

> Vobis M. Antonius nihil tribuit, clarissimis viris,
> legatis populi Romani: nos quid non legato M. Antoni Cotylae concessimus? (28)

Cicero keeps up the contrast in the next sentence:

> Cui portas huius urbis patere ius non erat, huic hoc
> templum patuit, hic hesterno die sententias vestras
> in codicillos et omnia verba referebat, huic se etiam
> summis honoribus usi contra suam dignitatem
> venditabant (28).

Conjugation, seen in the repetition of "hic" at the beginning of each clause, is a figure that one finds in Demosthenes (cf. *On the Crown* 221).

The thought that some consulars would "sell themselves" to Antony's agent leads to an emotional outburst
that acts as a transition to a brief discussion of how men
in public life should act:

> O di immortales! quam magnum est personam in re
> publica tueri principis! (29)

Some of these men, Cicero argues, think "nihil de dignitate, nimium de periculo"; and this leads to the question
"Quod autem est periculum?" which allows Cicero to introduce here a disjunctive contrast that we have seen so
often already:

> Nam si maximum in discrimen venitur, aut libertas
> parata victori est aut mors proposita victo: quorum
> alterum optabile est, alterum effugere nemo potest.
> Turpis autem fuga mortis omni est morte peior. (29)

The "nam" at the beginning of the next sentence introduces a thought that purports to be the reason for the
statement that precedes it, but in reality it is only tenu-
ously related to what precedes, namely, that no one should
envy those consulars who devote all their energy to defending the state. This, Cicero argues (30), is the duty of a
consular; and to buttress his point, he narrates the activities of Q. Scaevola the augur during the Social War. He
concludes this section, which is really only preparation
for the last section of the speech, with a defense of his

own activities, by tying together the last two ideas that are discussed in it:

> Huius industriam maxime equidem vellem ut imitarentur ei quos oportebat; secundo autem loco ne alterius labori inviderent. (31)

Once again in this passage, we see Cicero's ability to move quickly and subtly from one idea to the next, passing from the specific to the general and back to the specific again, combining criticism, argument, definition, elevated moral sentiments, and historical narration into a whole in which the ideas, in spite of the frequency of the transitional conjunctions "nam" and "autem," are only vaguely related to one another. The emotional impact of the section, however, is tremendous. As often in reading the speeches of Demosthenes, we are overwhelmed by the intensity, the rapid movement, the rush of the passage, which pulls us in every direction—from shame, to anger, to elevated conviction.

In the next section (32), we see Cicero's ability to repeat and elaborate upon points that he has already made, as Demosthenes usually does. There is first the idea that this is a conflict between freedom and slavery:

> Cum in spem libertatis sexennio post sumus ingressi diutiusque servitutem perpessi quam captivi frugi et diligentes solent. (32)

Consequently, consulars should shrink from no exertion to serve the state:

> Quas vigilias, quas solicitudines, quos labores liberandi populi Romani causa recusare debemus? (32)

This corresponds exactly to the definition of the duty of consulars that he had outlined in the preceding section of the speech:

> Summa laus consularium, vigilare [i.e., quas vigilias], adesse animo [i.e., quas sollicitudines], semper

> aliquid pro re publica aut cogitare aut facere aut di-
> cere [i.e., quos labores]. (30)

He then promises that he will conduct himself in accordance with this ideal ("Equidem . . . statui") and again criticizes those consulars who do not, especially those who
can tolerate Antony's treatment of the senate's envoys and
think that his envoy should be treated with honor:

> Non enim ita gerimus nos hoc bello consulares . . .
> partim ita a re publica aversi ut se hosti favere prae
> se ferant, legatos nostros ab Antonio despectos et in-
> risos facile patiantur, legatum Antoni sublevatum
> velint. (32)

Thus, in what could certainly be called a "subtle process of elaboration and development bringing to light new
dimensions of meaning and sensation,"[13] Cicero has re-
introduced in section 32 all the basic ideas of sections 28
through 31 and ends this passage with the idea with which
he began the preceding one. Cicero concludes the speech
on a calm note, with the proposal that all who desert Antony shall be pardoned and that all who join him after this
decree be considered enemies of the state (33).

This last passage also shows the same sort of stylistic
variety that one finds in the rest of the speech. There are
emotional outbursts, parallel constructions where appropriate, simple statements of fact. There is good use of repetition and polysyndeton for emphasis: "Nec vos ut legati
apud illum fuistis nec ut consulares, nec vos vestram nec
rei publicae dignitatem tenere potuistis" (28). However,
most of this passage, much of which consists of the exposition of Cicero's views and the defense of himself, is
written in the periodic style; and the sort of period he prefers is the analytical period often associated with Demosthenes. Here is an excellent example of the basically Demosthenic ability to state a simple thought and then
to spin out the ramifications and consequences of that

thought in clauses of varied length, especially the alternation of long and short clauses:

> (1) Non enim ita gerimus nos hoc bello consulares
> (2) ut aequo animo populus Romanus visurus sit
> nostri honoris insignia, (3a) cum partim e nobis ita
> timidi sint (4a) ut omnem populi Romani beneficio-
> rum memoriam abiecerint, (3b) partim ita a re pub-
> lica aversi (4b1) ut se hosti favere prae se ferant,
> (4b2) legatos nostros ab Antonio despectos et inrisos
> facile patiantur, (4b3) legatum Antoni sublevatum
> velint. (32)

The expansion, enlargement, variety, and cohesion of this period are typically Demosthenic.[14] The "ita" in the main clause foreshadows the first result clause (2), just as the "partim" following the "cum" leads the reader to expect another. Likewise, the "ita" in each of the two parts of the "cum" clause foreshadows the result clauses that follow. There is, moreover, considerable variety. The first result clause (2) is long. This is followed by the first part of the "cum" clause (3a), which is short and is completed by a fairly long result clause (4a). Likewise, in the second part of the sentence, the second part of the "cum" clause (3b), this time with no main verb, is short; and this is followed by a very long result clause (4b1, 4b2, 4b3), which, unlike the clause with which it is paired, is tripartite rather than simple, although the second and third parts of the clause are really just an elaboration of the first part. Like many of the periods in Demosthenes, this one alternately surges forward and contracts, moving back and forth between the general and the particular, only to enlarge itself at the end into a full completion of the thought, which gives weight and dignity to the end of the sentence.

Philippic IX is really the eulogy of Servius Sulpicius Rufus, who had died on the embassy to Antony, rather than an attack on Antony like the other *Philippics*. It is

written mainly in the "beautiful" style that is appropriate
to panegyric and shows many examples of Cicero's ability
to use the periodic style. The sentences in this speech are
more fully elaborated, especially by means of anaphora
and synonymity, than those in the preceding speeches;
but this type of elaboration is quite appropriate in a basically panegyric speech:

> Itaque non illum vis hiemis, non nives, non longi-
> tudo itineris, non asperitas viarum, non morbus in-
> gravescens retardavit, cumque . . . (2)

There are also many more examples of the suspenseful
period, even when Cicero is simply giving historical examples. Cicero preferred this type of period in his early
and middle speeches, with all the, often unnecessary,
elaboration that one also sees in these speeches, the style
that Hermogenes calls beauty. However, this is also more
appropriate in a panegyric speech than it would be in a deliberative speech; and Cicero seems finally to have realized that:

> Nam cum esset missus a senatu ad animos regum
> perspiciendos liberorumque populorum, maxime-
> que, ut nepotem regis Antiochi, eius qui cum maior-
> ibus nostris bellum gesserat classis habere, elephan-
> tos alere prohiberent, Laudiceae in gymnasio a
> quodam Leptine est interfectus. (4)

In spite of the elaborately periodic nature of most of this
speech, however, Cicero does know when to revert to a
simpler style to make a point emphatic:

> Non igitur magis Leptines Octavium nec Veientium
> rex eos quo modo nominavi quam Ser. Sulpicium
> occidit Antonius: is enim profecto mortem attulit
> qui causa mortis fuit (7). . . . Reddite igitur, patres
> conscripti, ei vitam cui ademistis. Vita enim mor-
> tuorum in memoria est posita vivorum (10). . . .
> Nec enim ille magis iuris consultus quam iustitiae
> fuit (10).

On the whole, however, the speech is composed in the full, abundant style that one often associates with Cicero, a style that he abused in his earlier speeches but learned to control in the *Philippics*. His return to that style in this speech is only another indication of his greater sense of propriety in the last years of his life, a sense of propriety, I would argue, that he had learned from Demosthenes.[15]

One might have expected Demosthenes' speech *On the False Embassy* to have been a model for *Philippics VIII* and *IX*. That does not seem to be the case, except in a very general sense, namely, the discussion that one finds in all these speeches of how a true statesman should act and the attempt to define what the role of a model statesman should be. The two situations differ not only from a historical point of view but from a stylistic one. Demosthenes' speech is a judicial speech and those of Cicero are deliberative, with panegyric overtones. Thus, the speech *On the False Embassy* is not really an appropriate model for these two *Philippics*.

At some time in the early spring of 43 B.C., probably at the beginning of March, Marcus Brutus informed the senate by dispatch that his own armies were in control of Greece and Macedonia, that Antony's brother Gaius was being besieged by republican forces around Apollonia, and that the proconsul Q. Hortensius was ready to turn the provinces over to Brutus as his successor, in spite of the contention by the supporters of Antony that Macedonia had been legally conferred on C. Antonius. When Pansa called a meeting of the senate to discuss whether the proconsulship of Macedonia and Greece should be formally conferred on Brutus, Q. Fufius Calenus argued that Brutus should be stripped of a command that he had seized by force. Cicero replied with the *Tenth Philippic*.

Some weeks later, news arrived in Rome that Dolabella was, in effect, in revolt against the senate. In the reallotment of provinces in April of the previous year, Dolabella had been assigned the province of Syria. As he was journeying to take up his command, he had to pass through the province of Asia, which was governed by Trebonius, a senatorial supporter who had been involved in the conspiracy against Caesar and who had been raising money and troops for Brutus and Cassius ever since he took up the command of Asia soon after the assassination of Caesar. When Dolabella reached the province of Asia, probably about the middle of January, Trebonius tried to expedite his passage through the province but refused him admission into Smyrna. Dolebella consequently took the city by force and put Trebonius to death. When the news reached Rome, Pansa called a meeting of the senate to discuss the prosecution of the war against Dolabella; and it was at this juncture that Cicero delivered the *Eleventh Philippic*, which, like the preceding speech, is concerned to a great extent with provincial commands. These two speeches, which are a good description of the situation in the east and the events that had transpired there in the late winter and early spring of 43 B.C., are therefore quite appropriate for a study of Cicero's narrative technique and the Demosthenic influence on it.

Aristotle observed that a narration was inappropriate and unnecessary in a deliberative speech (*Rhetoric* 3.13.3); however, Lionel Pearson has persuasively argued that one of the secrets of Demosthenes' oratory is the "constant emphasis on narrative in the *Philippics* and *Olynthiacs* (but always with an eye on economy of detail)."[16] Demosthenes realized, he maintains, that it was imperative in a deliberative speech to explain the political situation first: "If a political speech is to be effective, it must, no less than a forensic speech, contain some kind of *narratio*, some description of the situation or the problem which calls for a solution, in which its dangers are either emphasized or minimized."[17] In fact, Pearson argues, much of Demosthenes' success in general can be attributed to the fact that he used many techniques of forensic oratory, techniques he had worked out in his early judicial speeches, in his deliberative speeches, among them the frequent use of narration: "Without any hint at the beginning that he has found the right answer, he begins by explaining the situation and its dangers; the solution does not come until, as in a forensic speech, narrative and argument have prepared the ground."[18]

Moreover, in conjunction with this increased emphasis on narration, Demosthenes came more and more to react in a political situation as he would in a judicial trial: "The *Philippics* give us information, as the forensic speeches did; and the speaker seems to think of himself as facing a rival, not another Athenian politician, but Philip. . . . He also speaks constantly like a pleader in the courts who is concerned to show that someone is a dangerous and untrustworthy criminal, against whom the people must pass sentence by declaring war."[19] As in a judicial trial also, he wants to establish the defendant's motive as being the worst possible: "A criminal intention on the defendant's part is presented as the only explanation of his behavior."[20] Moreover, as in a judicial speech, there is constant emphasis in Demosthenes' deliberative speeches on the character of the opponent and the argument from probability that is related to it. In other words, he wants to make it clear that a man such as his opponent not only committed the acts that he attributes to him but was bound to act in such a way, given his character. Likewise, character depiction precedes the narration as in Cicero's judicial speeches,[21] so that the audience will be prejudiced from the outset and will interpret the "facts" as being consistent with the character depicted: "The speaker may pretend that the story reveals the main character, but he wants the jury to listen to it with their conclusions about his character already formed."[22]

All of this is a very good description of Cicero's narrative technique in the *Philippics*, as I will show below, especially in *Philippics X* and *XI*, which are composed mainly of narration. In these speeches Cicero, like Demos-

thenes, seems to have realized that "narration and interpretation of narrative were effective methods of explaining
matters of public policy, more effective sometimes than
appeals to principles and examples from the past."[23] Moreover, Cicero's stance in these speeches, as in all the *Philippics*, is very similar to that which one would expect to
find in a judicial speech; and this, like other aspects of
these speeches, contributes to the disjunctive nature of
the *Philippics*. Cicero is the advocate defending himself
or Decimus Brutus or Marcus Brutus against Antony's
supporters such as Q. Fufius Calenus, or prosecuting Antony or his brothers or Dolabella; like a good prosecutor,
he makes it clear that the defendant is wholly evil, a man
who could not have been reasonably expected to act in
any other way.[24] Indeed, in the *Philippics*, as in many of
Cicero's judicial speeches and Demosthenes' deliberative
speeches, character portrayal is often emphasized more
than the facts: "It is more important for the speaker to
convince the jury that the defendant and his associates
are undesirable characters, acting from discreditable motives, than to reveal what he may think are the true facts
of the case."[25]

As in a judicial speech, the first section of *Philippic X* is
devoted to setting the stage by establishing the characters
of the principal actors in the drama in such a way as to
prejudice the audience from the outset.[26] In the first sentence of the speech, Marcus Brutus is spoken of as a "praes-
tantissimus civis" who has brought to the state "maximum gaudium et gratulationem." Cicero then turns to a
criticism of Q. Fufius Calenus (3), who, in setting himself
in opposition to men such as Decimus and Marcus Brutus, finds no supporters in the senate and defends men
who are very different from himself and hated by all:

> Cur eos, quos omnes paene venerari debemus, solus
> oppugnas? . . . Quo est iste tuus sensus, quae
> cogitatio, Brutos ut non probes, Antonios probes;
> quos omnes carissimos habent, tu oderis, quos acer-
> bissime ceteri oderunt, tu constantissime diligas? (4)

Here, as often in the *Philippics,* again contributing to their disjunctive nature, Cicero tries to isolate his opponents as much as possible. He then asks Calenus whether he would want his own son to be like those whom he attacks or those whom he defends and answers the question for him: "Cur igitur non iis faves, eos laudas, quorum similem tuum filium esse vis?" (5). Cicero concludes this rebuke (6) with the observation that Calenus's only fault is this tendency to criticize good men ("plerisque in rebus bonis obtrectandi").

Thus, in this opening section of the speech, which takes the form of criticism of his opponent, Cicero's real intention has been to set the stage for the narrative that will follow. Having done so, he turns immediately to a description of the situation. Even this is the "tendentious kind of narrative of public events"[27] that is so characteristic of Demosthenes' later speeches:

> Legiones abducis a Bruto. Quas? nempe eas, quas
> ille a C. Antonio *scelere* avertit et *ad rem publicam*
> sua auctoritate traduxit. (6)

However, as in Demosthenes, narrative is constantly interspersed with argumentation, which often acts as a transition to the next point to be made. Cicero asks the senate whom it will ever honor if it decides to abandon Marcus Brutus, which leads him to a discussion of Brutus's role in the assassination of Caesar and allows him to continue the contrast between Brutus and Antony:

> Cui favebitis? nisi forte eos, qui diadema im-
> posuerint, conservandos, eos, qui regni nomen sus-
> tulerint, deserendos putatis. (7)

Cicero does not discuss the death of Caesar; it is too well known to need description. But he does narrate in detail the actions of Brutus after the assassination, details that support the description of his character that Cicero has sketched briefly earlier in the speech. In other words, as in Demosthenes, Cicero's use of narrative is "economical and he avoids unnecessary or irrelevant detail; he knows what can be left out and what must be included."[28] Moreover, in the emotional outburst that introduces the narration, again like Demosthenes, he recapitulates the portrait that he has drawn earlier:[29]

> Tantamne patientiam, di boni, tantam moderationem, tantam in iniuria tranquillitatem et modestiam! qui cum praetor urbis esset, urbe caruit. (7)

Cicero also handles his narration in a manner reminiscent of Demosthenes and Isaeus, from whom Demosthenes probably learned the technique; he knows "when to interrupt his story with a comment or explanation which can turn an incident into a powerful argument."[30] Although Brutus was praetor, "ius non dixit, cum omne ius rei publicae recuperavissct" (7). He was not present at the games that he had planned and sponsored, "ne quam viam patefaceret sceleratissimorum hominum audaciae" (7).

Moreover, Cicero is, as Pearson says of Demosthenes and Isaeus, "careful not to hurry ahead with his story before explaining the importance of an incident that needs some commentary."[31] He pauses to describe the goodwill of the people toward Brutus that was displayed at the celebration of the Apollinarian games: "Corpus aberat liberatoris, libertatis memoria aderat" (8). He then describes how he himself saw Brutus during this period, "nihil nisi de pace et concordia civium cogitantem," and witnessed his departure from Italy, "ne qua oreretur belli causa propter se," thus combining, as Demosthenes often does,[32] what he saw himself with a narration of what is general knowledge.

Cicero's description of Brutus's departure from Italy evokes an emotional outburst:

> O spectaculum illud non modo hominibus, sed undis ipsis et litoribus luctuosum, cedere e patria servatorem eius, manere in patria perditores! (8)

As in Demosthenes, "each emotional outburst is carefully motivated by descriptive passages which precede it. It is the timing of these appeals rather than any special art in their writing that we most admire."[33] Following this, there is a description of the departure of Cassius, and then Cicero brings the speech back to the point he wants to make:

> Exspectatum igitur tempus a Bruto est; nam quoad vos omnia pati vidit, usus est ipse incredibili patientia; posteaquam vos ad libertatem sensit erectos, praesidia vestrae libertati paravit. (9)

Cicero then turns, as a good dramatist should, from Brutus to his rival in the east, Gaius Antonius: "At cui pesti quantaeque restitit!" (9). Cicero first discusses the intentions of C. Antonius to gain control of Macedonia, Illyricum, and Greece so that his brother would have either a place of refuge, if he were defeated at Mutina, or a base of operations for attacking Italy. He then relates how Brutus foiled these plans, with the result that Greece now "tendit dexteram Italiae suumque ei praesidium pollicetur" (9), and expresses the hope that Antony will hear of this as soon as possible so that he will know "non D. Brutus, quem vallo circumsedeat, sed se ipsum obsideri" (10).

This acts as a nice transition to a paragraph describing the very difficult position in which Mark Antony now finds himself:

> Tria tenet oppida toto in orbe terrarum, habet inimicissimam Galliam, eos etiam, quibus confidebat, alienissimos, Transpadanos; Italia omnis infesta est; exterae nationes . . . civium imperiis et praesidiis tenentur. (10)

Ciccro has thus discussed in turn, with brief sketches, the three major characters in this situation: Marcus Brutus, Gaius Antonius, and Marcus Antonius. This speech, like those of Demosthenes, is "economical of detail, the characters of the drama are kept distinct, with only two or three of them in action at any one time."[34] He then sums up the situation in a tendentious narrative summary that brings together the three major characters (10--12): Antony's only hope was in his brother Gaius; if Gaius had gained control of Greece the situation would have been disastrous for the senate; Brutus, however, foiled his plans and has offered his support to the state; the senate, therefore, should confirm his command.

The final point is elaborated in the next section of the speech: "Quodsi ipsa res publica iudicaret, aut si omne ius decretis eius statueretur, Antonione an Bruto legiones populi Romani adiudicaret?" (12). This section relies heavily on narrative, as does the preceding one, although the purpose of narration in this basically argumentative section is more to support a specific point or to counter an argument than to describe generally the situation and the character of the major participants in it. Cicero's first point is that the senate should give the command in Greece to Brutus rather than to Gaius Antonius, and he supports it with a short narration of how each has conducted himself. Antonius had plundered and robbed Roman allies and Roman citizens; Brutus has protected them (12). The next argument is that the soldiers themselves have made it clear whom they support; and Cicero proves this thesis with a short narration (13) of the levy held in Macedonia by Q. Hortensius, the transferal of one legion to Cicero's son, the revolt of the cavalry from Antony's legates, and Publius Vatinius's surrender of Dyrrachium and his army to Brutus. This narration, which is simple rather than tendentious, leads naturally into a description of the general situation in the east at the time (14). These short but vivid narrations are well timed and well suited to the point they are intended to illustrate; and each argument is aptly illustrated before he moves on to the next. Cicero, as Pearson says of Demosthenes, "never remains in one position of attack for long, but moves around his various positions, strengthening each one in turn as he comes to it. . . . He uses the evidence of events with careful economy, not wasting time with unnecessary complexities or piling up one detail after another; his brief narrations are perfectly tailored to make the particular point that he wants to establish."[35] In many ways this careful timing and apt motivation, as well as the clear line of argument and the economy with which that argument is developed, are the most Demosthenic traits.[36]

This same approach is used to illustrate the next point, which, for the sake of clarity, is announced as usual at the outset of the argument, namely, that the state should not fear that Brutus will incite a war (14). This is proved by a repetition of Brutus's restrained and moderate actions after the death of Caesar, which involves a recapitulation, necessary in a long speech, of the earlier description of his character ("moderationem patientiamque"). Next, he meets the possible objection that the veterans and ex-Caesarians might object to Brutus's command by narrating (15–17) what support these groups have given to Decimus Brutus and by arguing that their attitude toward Marcus Brutus would be no different:

> Ergo illi certissimi idemque acerrimi Caesaris actorum patroni pro D. Bruti salute bellum gerunt; quos veterani secuntur . . . Quid est igitur, cur iis, qui D. Brutum omnibus operibus conservatum velint, M. Bruti sit suspectus exercitus? (16)

Thus, Cicero has described the characters of the major participants in the drama, he has clearly outlined the situation, and he has argued, by means of confirmation and refutation, for a certain point of view. Having thus prepared his audience, he is now ready for an emotional appeal similar to the kind one often finds in Demosthenes after a long section of initial preparation (cf. *Philippic III* 65–70). Cicero appeals to the sense of pride in his audience, an entreaty, like those in Demosthenes, that is "mo-

tivated with remarkable skill."[37] He has blackened his opponents and praised his supporters. He has described a
situation that is favorable to the senate and difficult for
Antony. He has brushed away all objections to his point of
view. Thus, having been won over by ethical and logical
appeals, his audience is ready to be inspired by emotion,
to be uplifted by the ideals of the orator himself. He has
discussed Brutus and Antony, the situations in which
they find themselves and the motives that inspired them;
now he himself will take the stage, as often happens in
the speeches of Demosthenes: "The narrative began from
Philip's point of view, then shifted to Aeschines; now it is
Demosthenes' turn to take the centre of the stage."[38]

The thoughts that inspire this section are those we
have seen before in the *Philippics*:

> Omnis est misera servitus . . . pro libertate vitae pe-
> riculo decertandum est. Non enim in spiritu vita
> est, sed ea nulla est omnino servienti. Omnes na-
> tiones servitutem ferre possunt, nostra civitas non
> potest. . . . Ita praeclara est recuperatio libertatis ut
> ne mors quidem sit in repetenda libertate fugienda
> . . . non est viri minimeque Romani dubitare eum
> spiritum, quem naturae debeat, patriae reddere.
> (19–20)

Like Demosthenes, Cicero seems "unwilling to abandon
an argument that he has used once, but when he uses it a
second time he may arrange the sequence of thought dif-
ferently."[39] Here the thought is developed in greater detail
than in the other *Philippics*, and the emphasis is on the
duty of every man to be willing to sacrifice himself for the
good of the state as much as on the preferability of liberty
to slavery. The presentation of this idea here is also more
general and more philosophical ("Non enim in spiritu
vita est") and appeals more vigorously to Roman tradition
("nos ita a maioribus instituti atque imbuti sumus") than
similar exhortations in other speeches.

Likewise, the tone of this appeal is more hopeful than we have seen before:

> Magna nos quidem spe et prope explorata libertatis causam suscepimus. (20)

And to reinforce this hopeful attitude, Cicero returns in the next section of the speech to narration. Here, in a straightforward narrative, he succinctly relates the events that have transpired in Italy since October of the preceding year, emphasizing the increasing difficulty of Antony's position:

> Concurritur undique ad commune incendium restinguendum. (21)

His conclusion is stated very simply at the end of the narration, where he again isolates his opponent:

> Unus omnium est hostis. (21)

This leads into a vigorous attack on Antony, his brother Lucius ("Quid illa taetrius belua, quid immanius?"), and his associates ("rustici atque agrestes . . . mimos et mimas"), in order to emphasize once again that they are dangerous criminals and generally wicked people. One sees here the basically Roman belief that character, in families as well as individuals, is constant; and this "proof from character" is essential to Cicero's narrative technique.[40]

He then returns to the point of the speech:

> Ad has pestes opprimendas cur moleste feramus quod M. Bruti accessit exercitus? (23)

To support his point, he sketches once again, in the full and emphatic style of panegyric, the character of Brutus:

> Omnis voluntas M. Bruti, patres conscripti, omnis cogitatio, tota mens auctoritatem senatus, libertatem populi Romani intuetur; haec habet proposita, haec tueri vult. (23)

This description, coming on the heels of that of Antony and his associates, a contrast that is another example of the disjunctive mode, is most effective. This is also reminiscent of judicial speeches and of the techniques of Demosthenes: "Speakers in the courts often contrast their own or their friends' tolerance with the violence and *hybris* of their adversaries, and this is the pattern of the present argument (*Phil.* III)."[41]

Then, having presented his case, Cicero makes a formal proposal (25–26) to the effect that Brutus and Hortensius should be praised and their actions should be officially approved by the senate. Like Demosthenes, he has prepared the ground for such a proposal through character portrayal, narration, argument, and emotional appeal, in such a way that no other opinion seems possible. As Pearson says of Demosthenes, "Before he makes any formal proposals, he wants it to appear that only a traitor could propose anything different."[42]

One sees the same characteristics even more clearly in *Philippic XI*, in many ways the most vivid, forceful, and dramatic of Cicero's speeches against Antony. Once again the character of the antagonists is drawn clearly in the first paragraph of the speech, and the dichotomy underlines the disjunctive nature of the struggle. Trebonius was a man of the highest character ("optimi civis moderatissimique hominis"). His murderer Dolabella and Dolabella's commander Antony are "capita . . . post homines natos taeterrima et spurcissima," in comparison with whom earlier Romans who were known for their cruelty—Cinna, Marius, and Sulla—seem almost humane (1).

At the outset of the speech, Cicero identifies Antony with Dolabella ("geminum in scelere par") and argues that there is a beneficial lesson to be derived from the cruel death of Trebonius:

> Ergo id quod fecit Dolabella in quo potuit multis idem minatur Antonius. (2)

Antony, he argues, is an enemy of all those who love freedom and, like Dolabella, plots cruel and unusual punishments for those who oppose him:

> Qualis igitur hostis habendus est is a quo victore, si
> cruciatus absit, mors in beneficii parte numeretur? (3)

Therefore, the senate should defend with even greater zeal than before the liberty of the Roman people:

> Eo maiore animo studioque libertatem defendite,
> quo maiora proposita victis supplicia servitutis
> videtis. (3)

To support his comparison, Cicero then narrates the actions of Antony and Dolabella, concentrating on those of Dolabella and making the point that the only difference between him and Antony is that Brutus had managed to restrain the furor of the latter (4–5). Cicero's description of the death of Trebonius is vivid and detailed, concentrating on the most gory aspects of the episode:[43]

> Post cervicibus fractis caput abscidit, idque adfixum
> gestari iussit in pilo; reliquum corpus tractum atque
> laniatum abiecit in mare (5).

Then Cicero underlines once again the fact that this is the sort of treatment that loyal Romans can expect from Antony:

> Ex quo nimirum documentum nos capere fortuna
> voluit quid esset victis extimescendum (5). . . .
> Imaginem M. Antoni crudelitatis in Dolabella cernitis. . . . Num leniorem quam in Asia Dolabella
> fuit in Italia, si liceat, fore putatis Antonium? (6)

To reinforce his point, he then returns to the description of Trebonius's death, trying, as before, to make the scene as present as possible, as Demosthenes often does (cf. *On the False Embassy* 196–99):

> Ponite igitur ante oculos, patres conscripti, miseram
> illam quidem et flebilem speciem, sed ad incitandos
> nostros animos necessariam: nocturnum impetum
> . . . vincla, verbera, eculeum, tortorem carnificem-
> que Samarium. . . . Ac Dolabella quidem tam fuit
> immemor humanitatis . . . ut suam insatiabilem
> crudelitatem exercuerit non solum in vivo, sed
> etiam in mortuo; atque in eius corpore lacerando
> atque vexando, cum animum satiare non posset,
> oculos paverit suos. (7–8)

Cicero's procedure in this first part of the speech very
much resembles that of Demosthenes: "As Demosthenes
developed his own style of political oratory, he learnt,
among other things, how to introduce narrative into political speeches and how best to draw the attention of the
public to what had happened and was likely to happen
again, if they were not careful and if they were not willing
to recognize the kind of people (like Philip) with whom
they had to contend."[44] Like Demosthenes, Cicero constantly emphasizes that men of the character of his opponents are likely to repeat what they have already done.[45]
The vivid detail of the vignettes, "whose brevity and ran-
dom cruelty have a sting that longer, more elaborate nar-
ratives would fail of,"[46] is also made more believable by
the carefully drawn character sketches that precede the
narration. As Pearson says of Demosthenes' approach:
"Details in the narrative that are not substantiated by evidence may be more readily believed if they fit into the pattern of behavior suggested by the character sketch. The
character is there for the sake of the narrative."[47] Because
of the importance of the character sketches, both Demosthenes and Cicero feel it necessary to "recapitulate and re-
elaborate the portrait at intervals,"[48] a technique basically
belonging to a judicial speech. Moreover, like Demosthenes, Cicero so cleverly blends arguments from honor
and expediency that the question at hand "seems not one

of advantage but of necessity, not the choice of a course of action but the adoption of the only possibility."[49]

The description of the death of Trebonius provokes an attack on Dolabella that is nicely timed and motivated, like all the emotional outbursts in the *Philippics*. The transition, moreover, is admirable:

> O multo miserior Dolabella quam ille quem tu miserrimum esse voluisti! (8)

The argument here, however, is surprisingly philosophical, involving the Stoic idea that it is better to receive injustice than to commit it. Since the mind is greater than the body, he who harms his mind is more sorely afflicted than he whose body is tormented (9). This is followed by a comparison, again rather calm, of the characters of Dolabella and Trebonius (9), again underlining the disjunctive nature of the opponents, who are presented as the embodiments of good and evil.

At the end of the attack on Dolabella, Cicero repeats the lesson to be learned from his activities, the a fortiori argument that he used before. It creates a nice transition to the next part of the speech, an attack on Antony and his other associates, and again underscores the importance that Cicero attaches in this speech to the nature of the adversary:

> A quo admoniti diligentius et vigilantius caveamus Antonium.
> Etenim Dolabella non ita multos secum habuit notos atque insignis latrones: at videtis quos et quam multos habeat Antonius. (10)

This section is composed of a series of attacks on Antony's colleagues that follow a similar pattern. In each case, the man is mentioned and then attacked with a brief narration of his former activities and a prediction, based on that, of how he will act in the future, similar to the argument used in reference to Antony:

> Quod horum consilium qui omnibus bonis hostes
> sunt nisi crudelissimum putatis fore? (12)

In this section, as in the preceding one, Cicero tries
to make his point as vivid and present as possible to his
audience:

> Quid? illa castrorum M. Antoni lumina, nonne ante
> oculos proponitis? (13)

And he concludes this section, as he concluded the attack
on Dolabella, with a repetition of the a fortiori argument
already used several times in this speech:

> Cum hanc et huius generis copiam tantam habeat
> Antonius, quod scelus omittet, cum Dolabella tantis
> se obstrinxerit parricidiis nequaquam latronum
> manu et copia? (14)[50]

Then, having prepared the audience with narration and
argument, presented in such a way that no other conclusion seems possible, as in the preceding speech, he states
his opinion, that the motion to declare Dolabella a public
enemy and to confiscate his estate should be passed. He
has prepared the ground well. The narration of Dolabella's activities, preceded by the interpretative character
sketches followed by the attack on the character of Antony's associates, which begins with the rather calm attack on Dolabella and ends with the really vicious one on
Titus Annius Cimber, creates a sort of crescendo effect
leading up to the statement of Cicero's own opinion; and
the repetition throughout of the a fortiori argument form-
ing the heart of this part of the speech is quite effective.

In the next major section of the speech (16–26), Cicero
deals with the question of who should conduct the war
against Dolabella. At the beginning of this section, we see
once more Cicero's ability to sketch out the situation
with a few rapid strokes of the brush, in the simple and
direct style found so often in the *Philippics*, and to focus
his attention clearly, rapidly, and precisely on what is at
issue:

Nunc, quoniam hostis est iudicatus Dolabella, bello
est persequendus. Neque enim quiescit; habet
legionem, habet fugitivos, habet sceleratam im-
piorum manum; est ipse confidens, impotens, gla-
diatorio generi mortis addictus. Quam ob rem,
quoniam Dolabella hesterno die hoste decreto
bellum gerendum est, imperator est diligendus. (16)

Like Demosthenes,[51] Cicero makes it clear at the outset of
the argumentation what his line of reasoning will be:

Duae dictae sunt sententiae quarum neutram probo:
alteram quia semper, nisi cum est necesse, peri-
culosam arbitror; alteram quia alienam his tempori-
bus existimo. (16)

One sees here, moreover, another important use that Cicero makes of narration in these speeches, the recount-
ing of historical precedent to justify a particular point of
view, as Demosthenes often does (cf. *Philippic III* 21–26).
Although this technique is not unusual in deliberative
speeches, it underlies Cicero's deep sense of tradition and
his tendency to interpret historical events in terms of patterns that have been seen in the past, which I will discuss
in greater detail in the last chapter.[52] It also illustrates
again the economy and rapidity with which he can make
his point in these speeches. In two sections of the speech
(17–18), he reviews briefly the major wars in which Rome
had been engaged from 280 to 83 B.C., emphasizing in
each case that it was not Roman practice to confer extraordinary commands on private citizens even in times
of great crisis. The variety of style in this section is also
admirable. It ranges from the well-controlled historical
period that we have seen before to the simple and direct
style so typical of many parts of the *Philippics*:

Bello Antiochino magno et gravi, cum L. Scipioni
provincia Asia obvenisset, parumque in eo putaretur
esse animi, parum roboris, senatusque ad conlegam
eius, C. Laelium, illius Sapientis patrem, negotium

> deferret, surrexit P. Africanus, frater maior L. Scipio-
> nis, et illam ignominiam a familia deprecatus est,
> dixitque et in fratre suo summam virtutem esse
> summumque consilium neque se ei legatum, id
> aetatis eisque rebus gestis defuturum (17). . . . Cum
> Aristonico bellum gerendum fuit P. Licinio L. Vale-
> rio consulibus. Rogatus est populus quem id bellum
> gerere placeret. (18)

All of the examples build up to the conclusion at the end:

> Otioso vero et nihil agenti privato, obsecro, L. Cae-
> sar—cum peritissimo homine mihi res est—quando
> imperium senatus dedit? (20)[53]

The next point that Cicero refutes is that the present
consuls should conduct the war against Dolabella, and
once again he relies heavily on narration. As often, he
makes clear at the outset what his position is: the crisis in
Italy is too serious to divert the attention of the consuls to
events in the east. The argument he uses to support this
attitude is a description of the situation in Italy that brings
together many of the points he has already made:

> Cum consul designatus obsideatur, cum a populo
> Romano pestiferi cives parricidaeque desciverint,
> cumque id bellum geramus quo bello de dignitate,
> de libertate, de vita decernamus, si in potestatem
> quis Antoni venerit, proposita sint tormenta atque
> cruciatus, cumque harum rerum omnium decertatio
> consulibus optimis fortissimis commissa et com-
> mendata sit. (21)

The conclusion is obvious in light of the situation: all the
attention of the consuls should be directed "ad virum for-
tissimum et omnium clarissimum liberandum" (22). Cicero, like Demosthenes, decided that a clear explanation of
the situation was the most convincing argument to support a certain point of view;[54] and, also like Demosthenes,
he tries to give the impression that only he has true in-

sight into the gravity of the situation and that what is needed first is to deal successfully with the most urgent problems:

> Nunc quod agitur agamus. Agitur autem liberine vivamus an mortem obeamus, quae certe servituti anteponenda est. (24)

In this section also, Cicero very successfully prepares his transition to the next part of the speech, as Demosthenes usually does:

> Quod si provinciae consulibus expetendae videntur . . . reddite prius nobis Brutum, lumen et decus civitatis. (24)

The end of the section contains a definition of sorts, which leads naturally into the next section of the speech, as in Demosthenes:[55]

> Expedito nobis homine et parato, patres conscripti, opus est et eo qui imperium legitimum habeat, qui praeterea auctoritatem, nomen, exercitum, perspectum animum in re publica liberanda. (26)

Having prepared the ground, he states his opinion at the outset:

> Quis igitur est? Aut M. Brutus aut C. Cassius aut uterque. (26)

Cicero also supports his choice by means of narration, a positive explanation of the situation expounded in such a way that the right course should seem obvious to everyone. First he describes in simple language the situation of Brutus in Greece and draws the only conclusion that one can reach from that description:

> Praeterea, patres conscripti, M. Brutum retinet etiam nunc C. Antonius, qui tenet Apolloniam, magnam urbem et gravem; tenet, opinor, Byllidem, tenet Amantiam, instat Epiro, urget Oricum, habet

> aliquot cohortis, habet equitatum. Hinc si Brutus
> erit traductus ad aliud bellum, Graeciam certe
> amiserimus. (26)

If Greece is lost, Italy herself will be threatened. Moreover, Cicero argues, once Brutus has subdued Gaius Antony, he will turn his efforts against Dolabella of his own
accord, even without a decree of the senate, since he has
always taken the initiative in defending the safety of the
republic. This latter trait he then proves with a brief narration of Brutus's former activities:

> Neque enim est in provinciam suam Cretam profec-
> tus: in Macedoniam alienam advolavit; omnia sua
> putavit quae vos vestra esse velitis; legiones con-
> scripsit novas, excepit veteres, equitatum ad se ab-
> duxit Dolabellae. (27)

Cassius likewise is motivated by the same spirit. In fact,
just as there was an identification earlier in the speech between Dolabella and Antony, here there is one between
Brutus and Cassius ("pari magnitudine animi et consilii
praeditus"). This section of the speech ends, therefore,
with a formal proposal that command in the east be conferred upon Cassius.

The rest of the speech is concerned with the advantages
to be gained from the proposal that has been made, just as
Demosthenes often devotes the part of the speech following his specific recommendations to a discussion of how
these proposals could solve the problems discussed earlier. Here again Cicero relies heavily on narration. He first
describes (32–35) the forces in the east that are ready to
aid Cassius and then relates Cassius's former activities
(35) as proof of his abilities and of his dedication to the
state. The end of the speech reaffirms the argument made
in the preceding *Philippic* that the veterans will not object to following a man who had been one of Caesar's
assassins.

One therefore sees in these four speeches how Cicero uses style and narration to give clarity, vividness, and "presence" to his oratory. In many ways, the immediacy of these speeches is their most compelling quality, and Cicero's adroit use of style and narration accounts most for their directness.

Chapter 7

The Rhetorical Situation
in the *Philippics*:

Philippics XII, XIII, and *XIV*

In the preceding chapters I have emphasized the influence that Demosthenes exerted on Cicero's *Philippics*. Oratory, however, is always evoked by a situation of some sort; it is a response to a problem that needs to be addressed. Thus it cannot be discussed solely in terms of internal influences on the orator; it must be viewed in light of the "rhetorical situation" that evoked it.[1] In this chapter, therefore, I will examine Cicero's *Philippics* as rhetorical responses to particular historical situations, paying special attention to *Philippics XII, XIII,* and *XIV*, which I have not discussed previously.[2]

A rhetorical situation has been defined as "a complex of persons, events, objects, and relations presenting an actual or potential exigence which can be completely or partially removed if discourse, introduced into the situation, can so constrain human decision or action as to bring about the significant modification of the exigence."[3] The most basic reality that faced Cicero when he made the decision to take up the challenge offered by Antony on 19 September was the fact of Antony's ascendency, both political and military. Despite his initial timidity and willingness to compromise, Antony had slowly begun to consolidate his power, and, as his power increased, he became less willing to compromise. Eventually, in the fall of 44, it became obvious that his aim was political and military supremacy.

After the death of Caesar, Antony had disarmed his opponents by agreeing to Cicero's compromise that the conspirators be pardoned in an amnesty but that Caesar's acts be confirmed by the senate and by his proposal that the dictatorship in Rome be abolished forever. By late April, however, he had begun to strengthen his position. He won over Caesar's veterans by a law that confirmed Caesar's promise of land to his ex-soldiers, and this gave him the support that he needed to get two laws passed by the tribal assembly in June, one giving him the governorship of Cisalpine Gaul for five years with command of the legions then in Macedonia and another putting into effect radical land reform, always a popular measure among the lower classes of Roman society. Then, in August, having gained military supremacy, he further increased his popular support with two judicial bills that were intended to make the juries more democratic.[4]

Having consolidated his political and military support, Antony began to repudiate the compromise that he had accepted after the death of Caesar. In early October, following his attack on Cicero, he called for a trial of Caesar's assassins and exiled them from Rome for the duration of his consulship.[5] Cicero stood by helplessly. Without military support, he realized, nothing could be done to oppose Antony effectively.[6]

Late in November, however, when Antony was making plans to get rid of the last obstacle to his political supremacy by having Octavian declared a public enemy, two legions defected to Caesar's legal heir. Cicero, who was always an opportunist, immediately seized upon the advantage that Octavian's support afforded and published the *Second Philippic*, which he had probably completed at least a month before.[7] Early in his career, when he was excluded from the *nobiles* because of his family background, he had supported the *populares* in the *Verrines* and the speech *On the Manilian Law* in order to advance his own career. Later, when he had been elected consul, he became a staunch supporter of the senate to ensure his own position. Now, he was willing to ally himself with parts of the Caesarian faction, which he later planned to discard, in order to reestablish his own position in Roman politics.

His most pressing concern was to rally support for the republican cause, to break Antony's political supremacy, as he hoped that Octavian would successfully challenge his military position, before it was too late, that is, before Antony became firmly established as governor of Cisalpine Gaul. We have already seen (chapter 6) that Cicero considered character depiction a necessary prerequisite to dealing with the situation at hand, and the primary aim of *Philippic II* is to establish firmly the character of the major participants in the conflict, very much like the first speech in the second action against Verres.[8] As in this speech and as in Demosthenes' *Philippics* and *Olynthiacs*, narrative is used to discredit the character of the opponent. There is nothing in the speech about what actions should be taken to oppose Antony, nothing about Cicero's own political program, no rational analysis of the situation. Emotional appeals are used to galvanize Cicero's supporters, and vilification of character is used to set the stage for the exposition of the specific proposals that Cicero would eventually make. These are seen, for the first time, in the *Third Philippic*.

Philippics III through *VI* were delivered in a situation of some urgency. In December Antony was marching north to occupy, by force if necessary, the province of Cisalpine Gaul, which Decimus Brutus was governing; and Brutus had declared his intention of resisting Antony. If Antony gained control of Cisalpine Gaul, Cicero realized, he would have an ideal base of operations for actions against the republican forces. It was imperative, therefore, that Cicero continue to galvanize those elements of Roman society that might support his struggle against Antony and that he convince the state to take some action to support Brutus. Thus, one can readily understand the prominence in these speeches of the vehement attacks on Antony, of the disjunctive mode—the attempt to polarize the conflict and to draw the battle lines as clearly as possible—and the *kairos* theme, the need for the senate to act quickly so as not to lose the advantage offered by the support of Brutus and Octavian. In other words, the situation that Cicero faced was very much like that presented to Demosthenes when hostilities broke out between Philip and Olynthus. Cicero also makes specific proposals: Octavian and the veterans who support him should be rewarded and honored, Brutus should be confirmed in his command, no negotiations should be conducted with Antony, who should be considered a public enemy, and a state of disorder (*tumultus*) should be proclaimed. In other words, having rallied support for his cause with the *Second Philippic*, Cicero attempts in *Philippics III–VI* both to consolidate this support and to begin to prosecute his political program against Antony in an attempt to break the military supremacy that was the real basis of Antony's power.

On the whole, these speeches were successful. The senate passed all his motions except the one proposing that Antony be declared a public enemy. However, despite Cicero's arguments against it, the senate did agree to send an embassy to Antony. Cicero realized that the opposition to Antony was not as firm as he had hoped. About the middle of January, therefore, during the absence of the envoys to Antony, he delivered the *Seventh Philippic*. This speech, unlike the previous four, was not evoked by any urgent crisis. The envoys were with Antony, and no action would be taken by the senate until their return. No proposals are made in the speech, and Cicero was speaking before an audience that he knew was basically sympathetic to his point of view. The only purpose of the speech was to firm up the opposition to Antony. Consequently, it is the calmest and most logical of Cicero's *Philippics*. In it he recapitulates, in a cool and orderly way, the basic arguments that he had used in *Philippics III – VI*, that peace with Antony was dishonorable, dangerous, and impossible. Like the preceding speeches, however, roughly half of this speech is directly concerned with Antony,⁹ which is a clear indication that Cicero's primary goal was still to isolate him and to alienate him from Cicero's own supporters as much as possible.

By the time that he delivered the *Eighth Philippic*, however, Cicero was on firmer ground; and he knew it. Antony had rejected the senate's terms and had sent back a set of arrogant demands, which caused most loyal Romans to rally around Cicero.¹⁰ He therefore turns his attention from Antony himself to Antony's supporters in the senate. There is very little in this speech about Antony; most of it is an attack on those senators who still felt that it was possible to avoid open war. In other words, Cicero felt confident enough about his own position to attack those in his own ranks who held moderate views.

Cicero's increased confidence is seen clearly in the next three speeches, which contain relatively little Antonian material. *Philippic IX* is really a eulogy of Servius Sulpicius Rufus. *Philippics X* and *XI* deal with the situation in the east and are more positive than the earlier speeches against Antony. These two speeches thus consist less of attacks on Cicero's enemies than praise of his supporters, whose actions they seek to have confirmed by the senate, and they deal primarily with positive steps that can be taken to strengthen the senatorial position. They exude confidence and assurance of final victory (cf. *Philippic X* 21; *Philippic XI* 39), unlike the tone of noble resignation to an honorable death that one finds in the earlier speeches (cf. *Philippic III* 35). These speeches are responses to actions that could only strengthen the senatorial position, namely, Brutus's assumption of command in Greece and Macedonia and Dolabella's murder of Trebonius, for Brutus was confirmed in his command and Dolabella was declared a public enemy and eventually crushed by Cassius.

In *Philippics XII* and *XIII*, however, Cicero is again on the defensive. During March, Antony's supporters persuaded Pansa to propose a second embassy on the grounds that Antony was now amenable to compromise. On the first day of debate on the motion, the senate seemed favorable; on the next day, however, the idea of a second embassy was opposed by P. Servilius and dropped. Cicero realized, however, that many senators were inclined to peace. It was at this juncture that he delivered the *Twelfth Philippic*, in which he vigorously argues against a second embassy or any compromise with Antony. Later in March, the senate received a letter from Lepidus, the governor of Nearer Spain, advocating peace. Since both consuls were at or near the seat of war, the senate was convened by the urban praetor to discuss the letter. Servilius proposed that Lepidus be thanked for his support but that it be made clear that any peace with Antony must be preceded by his agreement to lay down his arms. Cicero delivered the *Thirteenth Philippic* in support of this motion. He had been shown a letter that Antony sent to Octavian outlining his grievances, and much of Cicero's speech is devoted to a minute criticism of and violent attack on Antony's letter. In other words, at the time of the delivery of these two speeches, Cicero had perceived a growing inclination on the part of the senate and other Romans to negotiate with Antony and to compromise. Therefore, the aim of these speeches, in many ways the most unattractive of the *Philippics*, was to reverse that trend.

The first half of the *Twelfth Philippic* is devoted to a repetition of arguments that Cicero had used previously, especially in arguing against the first embassy to Antony in *Philippic V*: there should be no negotiation while Antony is under arms, an embassy would only serve to dampen the spirits of those loyal Romans who support the republic, true peace is not possible with a man like Antony (1–16). It is the second half of the speech, however, that is most interesting. Here Cicero talks about himself; and we see several traits that have been noticed before: his concern about his own reputation, his tendency to see situations in terms of polar conflicts, and his identification of himself with the state.

He begins this section by arguing that if there is an embassy to Antony he surely should not be a member of it:

> In hac ego legatione sim aut ad id consilium admiscear in quo ne si dissensero quidem a ceteris sciturus populus Romanus sit? Ita fiet ut si quid remissum aut concessum sit *meo semper periculo peccet Antonius, cum ei peccandi potestas a me concessa videatur.* (16)

Here it is obvious that Cicero's real concern is his own reputation, the defense of the extreme position against Antony that he has taken, which he reviews in the next two sections (17–18). One also sees here the way in which he identifies himself with the state ("a me concessa"), an idea that he develops more fully later in the speech.

Cicero also tries to arouse sympathy for himself by arguing (19–20) that it would cause him overwhelming sorrow to have to meet face to face with his most bitter enemy ("mihi uni crudelissimum hostem"). The use of the word *hostis* is striking and significant. It is usually applied to foreign enemies of the state, not to personal or political opponents, where one would expect to find the term *inimicus*; however, as he will make clear later in the speech, Cicero so identifies himself with the state that he considers his own enemies to be enemies of the republic.

It is clear, moreover, that his true motivation for not participating in the embassy is fear for his own safety, which he identifies with the safety of the state:

> Quid? vitae censetisne, patres conscripti, habendam
> mihi aliquam esse rationem? quae mihi minime
> cara est . . . vobis tamen et populo Romano vilis
> meus spiritus esse non debet. (21)

He then outlines in great detail, again an attempt to gain
sympathy, the many dangers that he would face if he went
on an embassy to Antony (21–30). He also further develops the point with which he will end the speech, the idea
that his own safety is inextricably connected with the survival of the state itself:

> Res declarat. Vicesimus annus est cum omnes
> scelerati me unum petunt. Itaque ipsi, ne dicam
> mihi, rei publicae poenas dederunt: me salvum ad-
> huc res publica conservavit *sibi* (24).

The "sibi," placed emphatically at the end of the sentence, is striking. And with this idea, Cicero concludes
the speech:

> Custodiatur igitur vita rei publicae mea. (30)

The way in which "rei publicae" is bracketed by "vita . . .
mea" is a verbal illustration of Cicero's point.

Cicero's tactic in this speech, as it was in the first half
of *Philippic II*, whose purpose also was to drive a wedge
between Cicero's supporters and those of Antony, was to
focus attention on himself, especially his importance to
the survival of the state, and to arouse sympathy for himself by emphasizing the personal danger that he has always risked in defending the republic (cf. *Philippic II* 1).
Both of these ideas, however, involve a more basic concept, which is crucial to understanding Cicero's *Philippics*: the identification of himself with the state and the
equation of his own survival with the survival of the
republic.

Philippic XII is quite similar to the first half of *Philippic II. Philippic XIII* is also very much like the second half

of that speech, the comprehensive attack on Antony's whole life. Nor is this surprising. The purpose of the *Second Philippic* was to rally support for Cicero's cause at a time when many Romans were willing to accept the supremacy of Antony, and its basic tactic is to focus attention clearly on the character of the two antagonists in the conflict.[11] Likewise, at the time of the delivery of *Philippics XII* and *XIII*, when the senate seemed inclined to compromise, Cicero felt the need once again to polarize the conflict as much as possible; and he resorted, as before, to depiction of character. *Philippic XII* he devotes to himself; *Philippic XIII*, which contains more Antonian material than any of the *Philippics* except the first two, is directed against Antony.[12]

In the first part of the speech, which is a reply to Lepidus's proposal for peace, Cicero repeatedly makes the familiar point that peace with Antony is not possible (2, 5, 16) and recounts some of the more memorable episodes of Antony's most recent career, namely, his offer of a crown to Caesar at the Lupercalia (17), his butchery of three hundred centurions at Brundisium (18), and his siege of Decimus Brutus (20–21). In a similar manner, he reviews his career in *Philippic II* to blacken his character. His conclusion is one with which we are familiar:

> Cum hoc, M. Lepide, pax esse quae potest? cuius ne supplicio quidem ullo satiari videtur posse res publica. (21)

It is in the second half of the speech, however, that Cicero most vigorously attacks Antony, by criticizing, almost line by line, a letter that Antony had sent to Hirtius and Octavian. The transition to this part of the speech is smooth:

> Quod si quis adhuc dubitare potuit quin nulla societas huic ordini populoque Romano cum illa importunissima belua posset esse, desinet profecto dubitare his cognitis litteris quas mihi missas ab Hirtio consule modo accepi. (22)

Cicero's attacks, many of them familiar from the other *Philippics*, are among the most vehement and vicious in all the speeches against Antony.

The bitterness and scorn of these attacks can be seen clearly from a few examples:

> In lustris, popinis, alea, vino tempus aetatis omne consumpsisses, ut faciebas, cum in gremiis mimarum mentum mentemque deponeres. (24)

> Lupercorum mentionem facere audet? neque illius diei memoriam perhorrescit quo ausus est obrutus vino, unguentis oblitus, nudus gementem populum Romanum ad servitutem cohortari? (31)

There are also attacks on Antony's supporters, filled with the sarcasm and bitterly humorous contempt that is so typical of this section of the speech:

> Est etiam ibi Decius, ab illis, ut opinor, Muribus Deciis; itaque Caesaris munera arrosit: Deciorum quidem multo intervallo per hunc praeclarum virum memoria renovata est. Saxam vero Decidium praeterire qui possum, hominem deductum ex ultimis gentibus, ut eum tribunum plebis videremus quem civem numquam videramus? (27)

The speech ends with the idea with which this section began and is a powerful statement of the disjunctive mode that we have seen so often before:

> "Prius undis flamma," ut ait poeta nescio quis, prius denique omnia quam aut cum Antoniis res publica aut cum re publica Antonii redeant in gratiam. Monstra quaedam ista et portenta sunt et prodigia rei publicae. (49)

The polysyndeton in the last sentence allows the orator to linger upon his attacks.

Cicero's attempts to repolarize the conflict with Antony, to harden the opposition, as he had done in the *Sec-*

ond Philippic, and to squash the efforts to make peace with him were successful. There were no negotiations, and the war was prosecuted by the consuls Hirtius and Pansa. On 15 April, Antony was defeated by republican forces under Pansa in what is often called the first battle of Mutina. On the twenty-first, the urban praetor summoned the senate to consider a motion by P. Servilius that civic dress should be assumed again and that a thanksgiving should be decreed. During the debate on the motion, Cicero delivered the *Fourteenth Philippic*, in which he opposed the first motion, on the grounds that the war against Antony was far from over, and supported the second, because a public thanksgiving, which had always been proclaimed to celebrate victory over foreign enemies, would be tantamount to declaring Antony a "hostis." The speech concludes with a eulogy of those who fell in battle.[13]

The speech is a suitable conclusion to Cicero's fourteen speeches against Antony, although there is evidence that there were other *Philippics* that followed it.[14] The battle of Mutina was the vindication of those policies that he had advocated during the previous five months. There was cause for celebration but also a need for caution, for Cicero realized that the war with Antony was far from over and remembered that his support in the senate for prosecuting the war to its conclusion was not as firm as he had hoped. The first major part of the speech (1 – 10) therefore urges the senate not to forget that Decimus Brutus is still under siege in Mutina (1 – 5) and demands, once again, that Antony be declared a "hostis" (6 – 10), another reminder that the war was not over.

The speech opens, somewhat unexpectedly, with a cautious suspenseful period reminiscent of the first sentence of Demosthenes' *First Philippic*:

> Sic, ut ex litteris quae recitatae sunt, patres conscripti, sceleratissimorum hostium exercitum caesum fusumque cognovi, sic, id quod et omnes

maxime optamus et ex ea victoria quae parta est
consecutum arbitramur, D. Brutum egressum iam
Mutina esse cognossem, propter cuius periculum ad
saga issemus, propter eiusdem salutem redeundum
ad pristinum vestitum sine ulla dubitatione
censerem. (1)

Then he states quite simply the reason for his caution,
mixing, as Demosthenes does, the simple and the complex:

Confectio autem huius belli est D. Bruti salus. (1)

Although the passage is cautious, it is characterized by
the sort of solemn and formal language that is appropriate
for the opening of a speech marking the successful completion of one stage of the conflict. There is anaphora, as
seen in the passage quoted above, synonymity ("cupimus
optamusque"), chiasmus ("animi virtus et spes victo-
riae"), and quite a lot of parallelism ("ne aut deorum im-
mortalium beneficium festinatione praeripuisse aut vim
fortunae contempsisse videamur"). Most of the sentences
are periodic.

However, the style becomes more argumentative in the
next section, where he demands that Antony be declared
a public enemy, showing clearly that, in spite of the good
reasons for celebration, the battle is not over. After a
very brief description of the battle, he makes his point
succinctly:

Si hostium fuit ille sanguis, summa militum pietas:
nefarium scelus, si civium. Quo usque igitur is qui
omnis hostis sclere superavit nomine hostis care-
bit? nisi mucrones etiam nostrorum militum tre-
mere voltis dubitantis utrum in cive an in hoste
fingantur. Supplicationem decernitis: hostem non
appellatis. (6)

This is followed by a rapid narrative, of the sort that we
have seen before, reminding the audience of Antony's
crimes, a prediction based on that narrative of how he

would treat loyal Romans if he were successful, and a comparison between Antony and Hannibal, arguing that Antony's crimes are fouler than those of Rome's greatest enemy (8–10). He dramatically recalls what the reaction in Rome was when the first rumors arrived in the city that Antony had been successful in the battle and asks the question: "Haec a quibus timebantur, eos hostis appellare dubitamus?"

In the second major part of the speech (11–25), Cicero turns to the proposal that a thanksgiving be decreed. Here too we see the mixture of optimism and caution that is typical of this speech and that was necessary, in Cicero's view, on this occasion. First (11–13) he supports the proposal and adds that the victorious generals, Hirtius, Pansa, and Octavian, be given the title "imperator." Then he digresses (13–21) to refute the rumors that he had planned to make himself "dictator." The real purpose of this section, however, is to continue to call attention to the dangers that beset the republic, especially those coming from Antony's supporters within the state, men whom Cicero calls "isti hostes domestici" (12). According to Cicero, it was these men who spread the rumor that he intended to assume personal power so that they would have an excuse to assassinate him, knowing that he was the only obstacle to their gaining control of the city (16). Here again we see the way in which Cicero identifies his own survival with that of the republic. He then describes the situation that makes his cautious attitude necessary:

> Cum alios male sentire, alios nihil omnino curare videam, alios parum constanter in suscepta causa permanere sententiamque suam non semper utilitate rei publicae, sed tum spe tum timore moderari? (17)

Addressing an unnamed opponent, probably Calenus, he restates the polar opposition that is so characteristic of earlier speeches:

> Aut, si ad me bonorum concursum fieri videbis, ad
> te improbos invitabis? (18)

Then, as is appropriate in a speech that marks the vindication of the policy he had espoused since late November of the preceding year, he rapidly reviews (19–21) his efforts against Antony. This leads up to the repeated demand, the third part of this section, that Antony be declared a "hostis." He supports this proposal with the argument, proved by a brief historical survey (23), that a thanksgiving has never been decreed in a civil war, only against "hostes":

> Supplicatione decernenda hostes eos, de quibus decernitis, iudicetis necesse est. (24)

In the third major section of the speech (25–38), Cicero praises the leaders (25–29) and soldiers (29–38) who fought against Antony.[15] However, even in this most optimistic part of the speech, he continues to emphasize the struggle for survival and the fact that the state has barely been snatched from utter ruin:

> [Octavius] qui primus Antoni immanem et foedam
> crudelitatem non solum a iugulis nostris sed etiam a
> membris et visceribus avertit. (25)

Like Demosthenes, he also emphasizes, to give confidence to his audience (cf. *Olynthiac II* 1), the idea that the cosmic forces in the universe support the republican cause:

> O solem ipsum beatissimum qui, ante quam se abderet, stratis cadaveribus parricidarum cum paucis
> fugientem vidit Antonium! (27)

> Quorum etiam nomen a Marte est, ut idem deus
> urbem hanc gentibus, vos huic urbi genuisse
> videatur. (32)

Therefore, the mixture of caution and optimism typical of this speech appears even here. Constrained by his experience of the previous six months with an often vacillating senate, Cicero tempered his triumph with cautious restraint.

One thus sees that Cicero's *Philippics* were responses to distinct historical or rhetorical situations and that he adapted these responses to the events that evoked them; and this, in addition to his own psychology and to the influence of Demosthenes, determined their nature. It is only in the context of the rhetorical situation that evoked these speeches and Cicero's own psychological makeup that we can truly understand how he manipulated for his own purposes the techniques of Demosthenic oratory that he had come to admire. These three factors, the rhetorical situation, the influence of Demosthenes, and Cicero's own psychological makeup, combined to produce a type of oratory that I have called the "rhetoric of crisis"; and that phenomenon will be discussed in the last chapter.

Chapter 8

Conclusion: Their Finest Hour

That there are similarities between the speeches of Demosthenes and Cicero's *Philippics* is clear. The most striking characteristic of these speeches is the polarization of the conflict into a dichotomy between good and evil, right and wrong, which is often simplistic in its approach. The orator sees the contest in which he is engaged as a fundamental crisis of the civilization that he represents, a crisis in which what is most good is pitted against what is most evil. This accounts for what I have called the "disjunctive mode" in these speeches and for the stance of advocate, defending good against evil, that the orator takes. This is also reflected in the images of struggling, usually for existence itself and often against overwhelming odds, and in those depicting the opposition between darkness and light, between order and chaos. This attitude also accounts for the orator's intractability, his refusal to compromise or to deal with the enemy, his demand for absolute victory or honorable defeat. His vision is static, fixated upon one goal; he is obsessed with the struggle and with victory, or at least that is the rhetorical stance he takes.

Related to this is a basically reactionary tendency of the orator to become a *laudator temporis acti* and the constant contrast in these speeches between the past, which is noble and good, which represents everything that is finest in Greek or Roman civilization, and the present, which is degenerate and unstable, mainly because of a degeneration of former standards of morality and patriotism. There is throughout these speeches a real nostalgia

for the simplicity and nobility that the orator sees in former ages and a vigorous attempt to inculcate into the audience attitudes and values of earlier generations. One
could call this the "myth of the golden age" applied to
politics; and the orator sees his major responsibility as
being a call to action, an exhortation to his audience to
put into effect the noble attitudes that they have inherited
from their ancestors.

In conjunction with this idealization of the past, the orator is prone to assume role-models and to see the crisis
that he faces in terms of patterns that have appeared in
the past. Demosthenes surely was inspired by the model
of Pericles[1] and saw the conflict with Philip in terms similar to that which had taken place earlier between Athens
and the Persian Empire. Likewise, Cicero, as has been discussed in chapter 3, modeled his own actions on those of
a whole series of earlier Romans and was always prone to
interpret each crisis in which he was involved in light of
an earlier pattern, the conflict with Catiline in terms of
the threat to the state from the Gracchi, Saturninus, and
Glaucia, the threat from Antony in terms of the conflict
with Catiline and Clodius (cf. *Philippic II* 1). Demosthenes was the last in a long line of political models that he
imitated; and the conflict between Philip and Athens was
surely the last of the historical patterns that he relived.

Also related to this attitude is a vehement defense of
traditional political institutions, which form a link between the present and the past and without which, according to Demosthenes and Cicero, liberty, freedom, and
participatory government could no longer exist. In other
words, the orator sees a necessary connection between
form and content. Without the traditional form, in his
opinion, the content would be lost.

The contest in which the orator is engaged, therefore, is
presented as a conflict in which the issue is survival, not
only of a particular form of government but also of the political ideals that such a form represents; and the desire to

save the system before it is too late accounts for the impatience and insistence on quick action that one sees in these speeches. The orator realizes, moreover, that he is defending a system without which his own role, his own political activity (and Cicero and Demosthenes were above all political animals), would no longer be possible; and this accounts as much as anything for the remarkable vigor and clarity with which he presents his case. Tremendous talent is coupled with the instinct for survival, the most basic of human impulses, to produce a form of oratory that is characterized by extreme clarity of vision, purposefulness, vividness, and rapidity of presentation, an oratory that is clean and direct and decisive, in which the organic synthesis of content, arrangement, and style is remarkable and striking.

Why these similarities exist is a more complicated question. As I have pointed out previously, there are resemblances in the psychological makeup of Demosthenes and Cicero; and this doubtlessly accounts for some of the similarities in their oratory ("Le style est l'homme même"). There was also a clear influence of Demosthenes on Cicero later in his life, and this is also an important factor in explaining the Demosthenic element in the *Philippics* of Cicero. However, there is a third factor, perhaps the most important, which must be taken into consideration, and that is the possibility that there is a special type of oratory evoked by certain historical situations, an oratory I have called the "rhetoric of crisis." This oratory is produced when an exceptional orator of genius and experience, working within a system that has a tradition of public address and public deliberation (that is, a democratic or participatory constitutional government), perceives, rightly or wrongly, that the very existence of that system and all it represents is threatened by a totalitarian menace that must be stopped at all costs.[2] This type of oratory, best exemplified in the ancient world by the speeches of Demosthenes against Philip of Macedon and by those of Cicero against Antony, has appeared at various times in the history of the western world when the conditions outlined above have been fulfilled. To take a recent example, in an attempt to illustrate more fully the existence of it, I would like to discuss briefly some of the speeches of Winston Churchill.

Like Demosthenes and Cicero in many ways, Churchill tried to arouse his fellow citizens to struggle with all their might against a tyranny that, according to him, threatened the very foundations of the British Empire and the way of life which that empire had produced and represented, a political system and a view of the world that was in many ways outmoded, like those that Demosthenes and Cicero defended. This is seen nowhere better than in the peroration to his speech in the House of Commons on 13 May 1940. Here, like Demosthenes and Cicero, Churchill makes it clear, in simple and direct language, that the issue is survival, not only of the British Empire but of all that the empire represents, again drawing a close connection between form and content:

> For without victory there is no survival. Let that be realized. No survival for the British Empire, no survival for all that the British Empire has stood for, no survival for the urge, the impulse of the ages, that mankind should move forward toward his goal.[3]

As in Demosthenes and Cicero, there is also an obsession with the struggle, and with victory; and the rhetorical pose that Churchill takes is to demand victory whatever the price may be:

> You ask what is our aim? I can answer in one word. It is victory. Victory at all costs—victory in spite of all terrors—victory, however long and hard the road may be.[4]

One sees also in this speech the "disjunctive mode" that is so typical of the speeches of Demosthenes and Cicero, the argument that this is a struggle between good and evil, and the cautious optimism that the cause of the orator will prosper:

> . . . and to wage war against a monstrous tyranny never surpassed in the dark and lamentable catalogue of human crime . . . I take up my task in buoyancy and hope. I feel sure that our cause will not be suffered to fail among men.[5]

Moreover, as we have seen in Demosthenes and Cicero, this optimism is buttressed by the conviction that the cosmic forces in the universe support the speaker's cause:

> To wage war . . . with all our might and with all the strength God has given us.[6]

Churchill's images, like those of Demosthenes and Cicero, reflect clearly the nature of the struggle as he sees it. His preference for archetypal images, especially light and dark metaphors, is indicative of the fundamental nature of the crisis as he depicts it.[7] One sees the simple alternatives that Churchill projects very clearly in the following passage:

> If we stand up to him [Hitler], all Europe may be free and the life of the world may move forward into broad, sunlit uplands. But if we fail, then the whole world, including the United States, including all that we have known and cared for, will sink into the abyss of a new Dark Age made more sinister, and perhaps more protracted, by the lights of perverted science.[8]

Here the many contrasts between light and darkness, the summits and the depths, the future and the past, progression and regression, freedom and slavery, underline the simple nature of the crisis as Churchill sees it, or at least as he wants his audience to see it.

One also sees in Churchill the idealization of an earlier

world that is temporarily threatened but that can be re-established once the threat is repelled:

> What he [Hitler] has done is to kindle a fire in Brit-ish hearts, here and all over the world, which will glow long after all traces of the conflagration he has caused in London have been removed. He has lighted a fire which will burn with a steady and consuming flame until the last vestiges of Nazi tyranny have been burnt out of Europe, and until the Old World— and the New—can join hands to *rebuild* the tem-ples of man's freedom and man's honor, upon foun-dations which will not soon or easily be overthrown.[9]

Here the whole concept of rebuilding an earlier society that was good but that is now threatened by a tyrannical menace is reminiscent of the nostalgia for the past that one sees in Demosthenes and Cicero.

How do we account for these elements in Churchill's oratory? One reason, as I have pointed out, is the nature of the crisis itself, which was similar to the ones faced by Demosthenes and Cicero. Another may be the psychologi-cal motivation of Churchill. I have suggested that the ora-tory of Demosthenes and Cicero was motivated by the will to survive and by a tendency to interpret situations in terms of polarized crises. Personal advantage and opportu-nism, rather than, or in addition to, pure patriotism, may have motivated Churchill as well. He knew that there would be no place in Hitler's new order of Europe for a man like himself, no opportunity for him to exercise those political and oratorical talents that were so respon-sible for his success. Like Demosthenes and Cicero, he also clearly had a keen sense of the dramatic and a pen-chant for crisis. Clement Attlee, for example, once ob-served that Churchill went around looking for "finest hours." And he found them, for in many ways he created them.[10]

Churchill was successful, but in spite of his success he could not save the British Empire that he had struggled to preserve. Like Demosthenes and Cicero, his success as a politician could be disputed; the quality of his oratory could not. The speeches that these men delivered, regardless of their motivation or their success, are remarkable examples of what Longinus called sublime oratory (*On the Sublime* 8). They are filled with noble ideas, inspired by vehement emotion and expressed in exquisite language; and the general effect is one of dignity, nobility, and elevation. The tools that they forged, quite apart from the political goals that they pursued, are their unquestionable contribution to Western civilization, for they are eloquent expressions of basic human values, always focused most clearly in times of crisis and upheaval, when traditional attitudes are questioned and rejected, values that represent the "unchanging essence of human identity."[11] They move us because they reflect an abiding faith that, in spite of superficial chaos and confusion, goodness and virtue, all that is best in man's nature, will one day triumph; and that is the essence of the spirit of humanism:

> For the morning will come. Brightly will it shine on the brave and true, kindly upon all who suffer for the cause, glorious upon the tombs of heroes. Thus will shine the dawn.[12]

Notes

For the speeches of Demosthenes and Cicero, I have used the Oxford Classical Texts: Demosthenes, *Orationes*, vol. 1, ed. S. H. Butcher (Oxford, 1903) and Cicero, *Orationes*, vols. 1 and 2, ed. Albert C. Clark (Oxford, 1905, 1901). The translations, unless otherwise indicated, are my own; likewise, any italics in quoted passages are mine. Section numbers from the above editions appear in the text in parentheses.

Chapter 1

1. The best ancient sources for the life of Demosthenes are his own speeches and those of his contemporaries, especially his rival Aeschines, and his biography written by Plutarch as well as the biography written by pseudo-Plutarch in the *Lives of the Ten Orators*. There are also biographies written by Libanius and Zosimus and scattered references in Photius and Suidas. The best modern work on the development of Demosthenes' political thought is Werner Jaeger, *Demosthenes: The Origin and Growth of his Policy* (Berkeley, 1938). Likewise, the best ancient sources for Cicero's life are his own speeches and letters and the biography written by Plutarch. There are also many good modern works on Cicero. I have consulted extensively the following: Frank R. Cowell, *Cicero and the Roman Republic* (Baltimore, 1962); Thomas A. Dorey, ed., *Cicero* (New York, 1965); Walter K. Lacey, *Cicero and the End of the Roman Republic* (London, 1978); Elizabeth Rawson, *Cicero: A Portrait* (London, 1975); D. R. Shackleton Bailey, *Cicero* (London, 1971); Richard E. Smith, *Cicero the Statesman* (Cambridge, 1966); David Stockton, *Cicero: A Political Biography* (Oxford, 1971). In preparing this chapter, I have relied heavily on the works listed above.

2. Martin van den Bruwaene, in his essay "Démosthène et Cicéron," in *Etudes sur Cicéron* (Bruxelles, 1946), says: "Démosthène garde à travers toute sa carrière quelque chose de dur" (80). On the whole, I do not agree with his eulogistic view of Demosthenes and Cicero, each of whom he calls "un martyr de la liberté" (80). George Cawkwell, *Philip of Macedon* (London, 1978), says of Demosthenes: "What he lacked in judgment he made up for in morose severity. . . . His whole temperament was nervous" (80). This trait was surely derived from his experiences in early life.

3. In May of 43, Cicero writes to Brutus about L. Clodius: "In eum autem locum rem adductam intellegit—est enim, ut scis, minime stultus—ut utrique salvi esse non possint; itaque nos mavult" (*Letters to Brutus* 1.1.2).

4. Cf. van den Bruwaene, "Démosthène et Cicéron," 106–7.

5. Helmut Rahn, "Demosthenes und Cicero: Zur Frage der geistigen Einheit der Antike," in *Atti del I congresso internazionale di studi ciceroniani*, 2 vols. (Rome, 1961), says that Demosthenes was a man inspired "aus dem attischen Geist der solonischen Eunomie und der Tragödie des Sophokles; Cicero aus dem der verklärten *maiores* und der *res publica*" (1:281); cf. also pp. 279–82.

6. Cicero says in a letter to Brutus written in April of 43: "Nec quidquam aliud decernitur hoc bello, nisi utrum simus necne" (*Letters to Brutus* 2.5.5).

7. Brutus seems to have felt that Cicero was motivated primarily by self-interest. In June of 43, he writes to Atticus: "Nimium timemus mortem et exsilium et paupertatem: haec nimirum videntur Ciceroni ultima esse in malis, et dum habeat a quibus impetret, quae velit, et a quibus colatur ac laudetur, servitutem, honorificam modo, non aspernatur—si quidquam in extrema ac miserrima contumelia potest honorificum esse" (*Letters to Brutus* 1.17.4). He also says in speaking of Cicero's activities: "Sed quaedam mihi videtur, quid dicam? 'imperite,' vir omnium prudentissimus, an '*ambitiose*' fecisse, qui valentissimum Antonium suscipere pro re publica non dubitarit inimicum?" (1). Brutus also implies that Cicero's struggle against Antony is a personal vendetta as much as anything. He describes Cicero's actions thus: "Sic patiamur, ut iam ista, quae facit, dominationem an dominum an Antonium timentis sint? Ego autem gratiam non habeo, si quis, dum ne irato serviat, rem ipsam non deprecatur" (2). Van den Bruwaene, however, says: "Cette propension à faire corps avec la cause semble être une des raisons du succès de chacun des deux orateurs" ("Démosthène et Cicéron," 82–83).

Chapter 2

1. The translation is by Stephen Usher in the Loeb Classical Library (Cambridge, 1974).

2. For some specific examples from *Philippics I* and *III* that illustrate this point, see Cecil Wooten, "A Few Observations on Form and Content in Demosthenes," *Phoenix* 31 (1977): 258–61.

3. Cf. Galen Rowe, "Demosthenes' Use of Language," in *Demosthenes' On the Crown*, ed. James Murphy (New York, 1967), 184–92.

4. For a general discussion of Hermogenes' work on style, see George Kennedy, *The Art of Rhetoric in the Roman World* (Princeton, 1972),

628–33. Some passages in English translation are given in Donald Russell and Michael Winterbottom, *Ancient Literary Criticism* (Oxford, 1972), 561–79; and a detailed treatment of the theory can be found in Dieter Hagedorn, *Zur Ideenlehre des Hermogenes* (Göttingen, 1964). The standard text is the Teubner by Rabe. Hermogenes' system is a conceptualization made five hundred years after the death of Demosthenes; and my use of it, therefore, is anachronistic in some ways. The main justification for using Hermogenes' system is that, unlike the theory of the three styles, which was developed at a time closer to Demosthenes' own, it works as a description of his oratory.

5. Rowe, "Demosthenes' Use of Language," 186; Gilberte Ronnet, *Etude sur le style de Démosthène dans les discours politiques* (Paris, 1951), 182, 186.

6. Galen Rowe, "Demosthenes' *First Philippic*: The Satiric Mode," *Transactions of the American Philological Association* 99 (1968): 362. For some discussion and examples of the way in which Demosthenes holds a long speech together, see Cecil Wooten, "The Nature of Form in Demosthenes' *de Corona*," *Classical World* 72 (1979): 321–27.

7. See Lionel Pearson, "The Development of Demosthenes as a Political Orator," *Phoenix* 18 (1964): 95–109.

8. I give the following examples. In the speech *On the Crown*, he describes his role in politics as that of a soldier taking up his post (62) and describes Philip's taking of Elateia as a "danger besieging the city" (188). In *Philippic I* he speaks of Philip as always casting a net around the Athenians (9). In *Philippic III* he speaks of Philip as a disease (29) and of Greece as "being sick" (39). These medical images are especially closely related to the thought because Demosthenes felt that Athens could be "cured" if the Athenians would take the preventive medicine that he was prescribing; see Cecil Wooten, "Unnoticed Medical Language in Demosthenes," *Hermes* 107 (1979): 157–60. In *Philippic III* (33) Philip is compared to a hailstorm over which no one has any control, and in the speech *On the Crown* (288) Demosthenes says that the danger arising from Philip's seizure of Elateia vanished "like a cloud" when his proposals were passed.

9. He compares the Athenians to a Persian boxer who fights defensively only (*Philippic I* 40). In the speech *On the Crown* (194), he compares himself to a shipowner who did everything in his power to ensure the safety of his ship but who could not foresee the great storm that it would encounter. Philip, like bad weather, was a force over which men had little control. In this same speech (243), he compares Aeschines, his rival, to a doctor who refuses to prescribe while the patient is sick but has advice to give after he is dead. Certain images are seen throughout this speech. Images of buying and selling are intended to underline Aeschines' venality. The images of physical pollution and disease rein-

force this idea of his rival's corruption and the idea that the whole state was corrupted by Philip. Demosthenes portrays himself as the doctor. Images portraying Athens as a ship and Philip as a storm over which she had no control are also frequent. (It is interesting to note that in the similes in the speeches delivered before Philip's defeat of Athens in 338 the Athenians are generally depicted as a force that had control over its destiny, that could ward off destruction if only it would take action. In the speech *On the Crown*, however, the Athenians are generally depicted as a passive force, which had no real control over its destiny. These images are obviously intended to ingratiate Demosthenes with his audience by minimizing their role in the defeat of Athens.) This repetition of certain images is typical of Demosthenes' style and is intended to plant certain concepts deeply in the minds of his listeners through a recurrence of certain motifs. The repetition of these motifs is really what holds this long speech together. Cf. Cecil Wooten, "La Funzione delle metafore e delle similitudini nelle orazioni di Demostene," *Quaderni Urbinati* 29 (1978): 123–25; and "The Nature of Form," 326–27.

10. See Ronnet, *Etude sur le style de Démosthène,* 149–82, for a very good discussion of Demosthenes' similes and metaphors in general.

11. See Rowe, "Demosthenes' Use of Language," 184. Here, for example, he separates the balanced sentences by an intervening thought. This addition of a brief explanation following a longer statement is typical of Demosthenes, as is his alternation of long and short statements in the third and fourth sentences. In the second of the contrasted sentences, he uses two verbs in the main clause and adds a participial phrase, neither of which appears in the first sentence.

12. See Ronnet, *Etude sur le style de Démosthène,* 55–62.

13. Demosthenes often uses hyperbaton, the separation of words that naturally go together, in conjunction with synonymity, to give even more emphasis to the elements involved: "I ask, men of Athens, and I beg . . ." (*On the Crown* 34).

14. Like synonymity is enumeration, the listing of components of a general term; it too is intended to call attention to the idea and to add weight and majesty to the style: "Let him consider, however, that we once, gentlemen of Athens, held Pydna and Potidaea and Methone and all the territory surrounding his kingdom" (*Philippic I* 4). The last term in the enumeration, as here, often sums up the list.

15. For a remarkable example of this, see Wooten, "A Few Observations," 258.

16. Cf. the discussion in Longinus, *On the Sublime* 18, 1–2.

17. Annabel Patterson, *Hermogenes and the Renaissance* (Princeton, 1970), 107.

18. Ronnet, *Etude sur le style de Démosthène,* 83–102.

19. Patterson, *Hermogenes and the Renaissance,* 123.

20. Ibid., 186. Chaim Perelman and Lucie Olbrechts-Tyteca point out in *The New Rhetoric: A Treatise on Argumentation*, trans. John Wilkinson and Purcell Weaver (Notre Dame, 1969), that "the most effective eloquence is the eloquence which appears to be the normal consequence of a situation" (451).

21. Patterson, *Hermogenes and the Renaissance*, 33.

22. George Kennedy, "Focusing of Arguments in Greek Deliberative Oratory," *Transactions of the American Philological Association* 90 (1959): 131–38.

23. In his use of historical parallels and contrasts, Demosthenes, like all the Attic orators, is careful not to be overly precise or to appear overly learned so as not to alienate his audience. He gives the impression that his knowledge of history comes from hearsay or general report. See Lionel Pearson, "Historical Allusions in the Attic Orators," *Classical Philology* 58 (1963): 109–11.

24. One sees quite well in the speech *On the Crown* how effectively Demosthenes could combine narration and argumentation. In this speech he quite often relates a historical event, then conjectures a course of action that might appear to have been more desirable, and finally argues that the action taken was more beneficial or the only option in keeping with Athenian traditions. See Donovan J. Ochs, "Demosthenes' Use of Argument," in *Demosthenes' On the Crown*, ed. James Murphy, p. 168.

Chapter 3

1. See George Kennedy, *The Art of Rhetoric in the Roman World* (Princeton, 1972), 147, 278.

2. See Elizabeth Rawson, *Cicero: A Portrait* (London, 1975), 12–14. For a more extensive treatment of this question, see Thomas N. Mitchell, *Cicero: The Ascending Years* (New Haven, 1979).

3. I do not mean that there may not have been occasional imitations; cf. Lionel Pearson, "Cicero's Debt to Demosthenes in the *Verrines*," *Pacific Coast Philology* 3 (1968): 49–54. Alfons Weische, *Ciceros Nachahmung der attischen Redner* (Heidelberg, 1972), 171–78, discusses the differences between Cicero and Demosthenes in Cicero's early speeches. That Cicero knew and had studied Demosthenes' oratory extensively in his youth cannot be disputed (cf. Weische, 137–40).

4. Cf. Kennedy, *Art of Rhetoric*, 164, 173–82; Robin G. M. Nisbet, "The Speeches," in *Cicero*, ed. Thomas A. Dorey (New York, 1965), 62–63; Eduard Norden, *Die Antike Kunstprosa*, 2 vols. (Leipzig, 1909), 1 : 225–33. Cicero, moreover, thinks of style in terms of the neat categories that were taught in the schools: the plain, the middle, and the grand.

Where Cicero does try to vary the style, he seems to think of "discrete entities within the oration" (the phrase is used by Galen Rowe, "Demosthenes' Use of Language," in *Demosthenes' On the Crown*, ed. James Murphy [New York, 1967], 192) rather than a merger of all these styles in a flexible and fluid whole with the subtle variations of which Demosthenes was capable. The Catilinarians, however, are examples of "the rhetoric of crisis"; and I will return to a consideration of them in a note to the last chapter.

5. However, it is obviously not my purpose here to disprove that Cicero was modeling his oratory on that of Demosthenes. That has never really been seriously argued. I am simply trying to show the differences in technique. I cannot accept Eric Laughton's thesis, which is developed briefly in his article "Cicero and the Greek Orators," *American Journal of Philology* 82 (1961): 27–49, that Cicero's style was indebted to Demosthenes throughout his life. Laughton deals with only three passages from Cicero and treats only three aspects of his style, "progressive rhythm" (45), synonymity, and asyndeton. Synonymity and asyndeton are common stylistic features, used to a certain extent by all orators; it would be rash, I think, to see in Cicero's use of them the influence of Demosthenes. His point about the "progressive movement and expansion" (48) that is characteristic of the Ciceronian and Demosthenic period is better taken but still inconclusive. Isocrates' periods are not as rambling as Laughton would have one believe; see Richard C. Jebb, *The Attic Orators from Antiphon to Isaeus*, 2 vols. (London, 1893), 2:62–63. Moreover, what is truly Isocratean about Cicero's use of the period is his abuse of the periodic style, his tendency to overuse it, which Demosthenes never did (Rowe, "Demosthenes' Use of Language," 189). Also, I hope to show that Cicero did not always admire Demosthenic style, which Laughton takes for granted.

6. Robert Y. Tyrrell, *The Correspondence of M. Tullius Cicero* (Dublin, 1885), brackets this passage; it is accepted, however, by D. R. Shackleton Bailey, *Cicero's Letters to Atticus* (Cambridge, 1965). Cicero here is talking not about a change of style but a change to a different branch of oratory, deliberative rather than forensic.

7. *On Oratory* 1.58, 89, 260; *On Oratory* 3.28, 71, 213; Cf. Emanuele Castorina, *L'Ultima oratoria di Cicerone* (Catania, 1975), 28–37.

8. Cf. Harry Hubbell, *The Influence of Isocrates on Cicero, Dionysius, and Aristides* (New Haven, 1914); Harry Hubbell, "Cicero on Styles of Oratory," *Yale Classical Studies* 19 (1966): 171–86; Jebb, *Attic Orators*, 2:72–73; Henry Nettleship, *Passages for Translation into Latin Prose* (London, 1887), 49–55; Kennedy, *Art of Rhetoric*, 279; John E. Sandys, ed., *Orator* (Cambridge, 1885), xxii, xxxiii; Norden, *Die Antike Kunstprosa*, 1:226.

9. These three categories are first mentioned in the *Rhetoric to Gaius*

Herennius 4, 8. See the note in Harry Caplan's edition in the Loeb Classical Library (Cambrdige, 1954), 252–53.

10. *On the Best Kind of Orators* 6, 10, 13, 14, 17, 19–21; *Orator* 6, 15, 23, 26–27, 29, 56, 90, 104–5, 110, 133, 136, 151, 226, 234; *Brutus* 35, 66, 121, 138, 141, 191, 285, 288–91.

11. *On the Best Kind of Orators* 13; *Orator* 6, 23, 26, 104; *Brutus* 35, 141, 288, 291.

12. Cicero also hit upon Demosthenes' one great weakness, his lack of humor; however, he tries to turn even this into a compliment by arguing that although Demosthenes was not *dicax* (witty) he was *facetus* (humorous), which Cicero calls a greater art (*Orator* 90).

13. This is quite clear from a passage in the *Third Philippic* 34–36; cf. also *Letters to Friends* 12.2.1.

14. It is not completely clear whether the word *fulmina* in *Letters to Friends* (9.21) is Cicero's own or a quotation from the letter written to him by Papirius Paetus. The phrase "meorum verborum, ut scribis, fulmina" (1) could well mean that the phrase had been used by Papirius Paetus. In "Cicero and the Greek Orators," however, Laughton comes to the same conclusion as I do. He says: "As Demosthenes had used his eloquence as a weapon against Philip, so Cicero imagined himself if ever the opportunity came, standing forth against Antony as champion of all loyal elements in Rome. It seems probable that from such thoughts as these, in the early summer of 44 B.C., was born the title 'Philippics' which he subsequently gave to the series of speeches against Antony which began later in the same year" (36).

15. John D. Denniston, in his introduction to the commentary on *Philippics I* and *II* (Oxford, 1926), says: "It must be admitted that the title *Philippics* is not a very happy one. If we are to look for a Demosthenic parallel, the *De Corona*, in spite of many differences, resembles at any rate the *Second Philippic* more closely. Both speeches contain an elaborate defense of the author's whole political career, delivered near its close: and both combine this defense with a fierce and virulent attack on the career of the political opponent" (xvii). I have chosen not to treat the *First Philippic* since it was delivered before the final break with Antony and, consequently, before Cicero realized what was at stake in this contest.

16. Cf. Cecil Wooten, "The Nature of Form in Demosthenes' *de Corona*," *Classical World* 72 (1979): 321–27.

17. Kennedy, *Art of Rhetoric*, 258.

18. This is Weische's attitude. He says: "Aber man könnte fragen, ob nicht die Philippischen Reden Ciceros ein argument dafür sind, dass er in den letzten Jahren seines Lebens eine neue Nähe zu Demosthenes erreicht habe. Darauf ist zu antworten, dass die Zahl der Nachahmungen einzelner Demosthenesstellen in den Philippischen Reden im ganzen

nicht zugenommen hat" (*Ciceros Nachahmung*, 193). Eric Laughton, *The Participle in Cicero* (Oxford, 1964), points out, however, the increased number of Grecisms in Cicero's later writings, especially the letters and philosophical treatises (43).

19. Cf. Donat Joseph Taddeo, "Signs of Demosthenes in Cicero's Philippics" (Ph.D. diss., Stanford University, 1971), iii.

20. Cf. *On the Crown* 125; *Philippic II* 2, 10–12, 16, 18, 51. As Weische points out, Cicero seems to be indicating at the outset of his speech the model that he is following (*Ciceros Nachahmung*, 100, 194).

21. Cf. *On the Crown* 9–125; *Philippic II* 3–42.

22. Cf. *On the Crown* 126–296; *Philippic II* 44–115.

23. Cf. Taddeo, "Signs of Demosthenes," 33, 37, 40, 42. For Cicero's use of characterization, see Richard McClintock, "Cicero's Narrative Technique in the Judicial Speeches" (Ph.D. diss., University of North Carolina, 1975), 41, 50, 60, 139, 157, 172–73.

24. This is true of almost all the *Philippics*; see Marcel Delaunois, "Statistiques des idées dans le cadre du plan oratoire des *Philippiques* de Cicéron," *Les Etudes Classiques* 34 (1966): 3–34.

25. Cf. Taddeo, "Signs of Demosthenes," 43, 46, 48, 52, 56–57, 59. It is interesting to note, moreover, that Cicero incorporates into his speech Demosthenes' most prevalent argument, that his opponent should have made his charges when the matter was a national issue (cf. *Philippic II* 23, 31; and Francis P. Donnelly, "The Argument Used Seventy-two Times in the *Crown Speech* of Demosthenes," *Classical World* 28 [1935]: 153–56).

26. *Philippic II* 63, 76, 84, 104.

27. Cf. Rowe's discussion of these images in "Demosthenes' Use of Language," 178.

28. *Philippic II* 55; *On the Crown* 159. See Laughton, "Cicero and the Greek Orators": "As for the *De Corona*, at the risk of seeming fanciful, I will venture to express a belief that, if one had the time and patience to acquire a sufficiently detailed and verbal knowledge both of the *De Corona* and of Cicero's last series of public speeches, the *Philippics*, one might collect a considerable number of parallelisms of thought and expression similar to that which commentators have long noted between *De Corona* 59 and *Philippic* II, 55" (34–35). Weische does just this. He points out the similarity in structure between *On the Crown* 198 and *Philippic II* 55 (*Ciceros Nachahmung*, 103). Both orators use a pattern consisting of statement, antistrophe, simile, and recapitulation. In the last sentence in each case, the first clause has no verb and the opponent is at the end. There is also a similarity in the thought at *On the Crown* 143 and *Philippic II* 55, the idea that one man is responsible for the woes of the state.

29. Nettleship, *Passages for Translation*, 53; Nisbet, "The Speeches,"

76; Louis Laurand, "Sur l'évolution de la langue et du style de Cicéron," *Revue de Philologie* 7 (1933): 67; Rowe, "Demosthenes' Use of Language," 198–99. See also Karl Büchner, *Cicero: Bestand und Wandel seiner geistigen Welt* (Heidelberg, 1964), 508.

30. Ralph Johnson, *Luxuriance and Economy: Cicero and the Alien Style* (Berkeley, 1971).

31. Johnson, *Luxuriance and Economy*, 38. Cf. Gilberte Ronnet, *Etude sur le style de Démosthène dans les discours politiques* (Paris, 1951), 182, 186.

32. Ibid., 45, 46, 59, 60.

33. Rowe, "Demosthenes' Use of Language," 199.

34. Johnson, *Luxuriance and Economy*, 45; quoted passage is from p. 46.

35. Rowe, "Demosthenes' Use of Language," 186, 189; Ronnet, *Etude sur le style de Démosthène*, 183–86; Jebb, *Attic Orators*, 2:308–9.

36. Johnson, *Luxuriance and Economy*, 39.

37. Rowe, "Demosthenes' Use of Language," 186; Ronnet, *Etude sur le style de Démosthène*, 101.

38. Johnson, *Luxuriance and Economy*, 61.

39. It should be noted that this general period saw a lot of interest in Demosthenes' style. Not long after Cicero's death, Dionysius of Halicarnassus wrote his essay on Demosthenes' style, and this may reflect the interest of earlier critics such as Caecilius of Calacte. These stylistic analyses became increasingly more subtle and eventually led to the work of Hermogenes discussed in the preceding chapter. It is also interesting that Atticus's publishing house issued an edition of Demosthenes; see A. F. von Pauly and Georg Wissowa, *Paulys Real-Encyclopädie der classischen Altertumswissenschaft* (Stuttgart, 1894–), pt. II A, vol. 1, 698.

Chapter 4

1. Cf. Donat Joseph Taddeo, "Signs of Demosthenes in Cicero's Philippics" (Ph.D. diss., Stanford University, 1971), 1–2.

2. Cf. Cecil Wooten, "Cicero's Reactions to Demosthenes: A Clarification," *Classical Journal* 73 (1977): 37–41.

3. As has been pointed out, there are very few passages in Cicero's *Philippics* in which he seems to be copying Demosthenes closely. What I am going to discuss is how Cicero may have let himself be inspired, in a more general way, by Demosthenic techniques of developing and presenting themes and arguments; cf. Taddeo, "Signs of Demosthenes," iii.

4. Cf. *Philippic IV* 11–12. This is what Chaim Perelman and Lucie Olbrechts-Tyteca, in their book *The New Rhetoric: A Treatise on Argumentation*, trans. John Wilkinson and Purcell Weaver (Notre Dame,

1969), call the "locus of the irreparable" (92). For a brief discussion of the "paranoid style" in Demosthenes, see Cecil Wooten, "The Nature of Form in Demosthenes' *de Corona,*" *Classical World* 72 (1979): n. 28.

5. The position of "nullam," separated from the noun that it modifies and put toward the end of the sentence, is very emphatic.

6. This is very well discussed by Taddeo, "Signs of Demosthenes," 1–7, 18, 22–23.

7. See Lionel Pearson, "The Development of Demosthenes as a Political Orator," *Phoenix* 18 (1964): 95–109; and Friedrich Blass, *Die Attische Beredsamkeit,* 3 vols. (Leipzig, 1893), 3:437.

8. This is surely the Latin for the Greek *kairos,* as is the use of "occasio" above; see Taddeo, "Signs of Demosthenes," 28.

9. Cicero's ability to resist rhetorical elaboration here, especially extreme parallelism or chiasmus, makes the elegant simplicity of this sentence even more moving. In fact, as has been pointed out, in the *Philippics* Cicero generally uses a simpler, more direct, and more Demosthenic sentence structure than in his earlier speeches.

10. Cf. August Imholtz, "Gladiatorial Metaphors in Cicero's *Pro Sex. Roscio Amerino,*" *Classical World* 65 (1972): 228–30. For a discussion of the a fortiori argument, see Cicero, *Topica* 68.

11. For a discussion of this type of argument, see Cicero, *Topica* 56–57; and Edward P. J. Corbett, *Classical Rhetoric for the Modern Student* (New York, 1965), 59, 75, 116–19. Corbett refers to this as the "black-or-white syndrome" (75). Christopher P. Craig, "The Role of Rational Argumentation in Selected Judicial Speeches of Cicero" (Ph.D. diss., University of North Carolina, 1979), points out that this type of argument is unusual in Cicero and first appears in the speech *For Milo* (238).

12. George Kennedy, *The Art of Persuasion in Greece* (Princeton, 1963), 224–25.

13. Taddeo, "Signs of Demosthenes," 23–25.

14. Cf. Gilberte Ronnet, *Etude sur le style de Démosthène dans les discours politiques* (Paris, 1951), 149–82.

15. For the use of characterization as argument, see Richard McClintock, "Cicero's Narrative Technique in the Judicial Speeches" (Ph.D. diss., University of North Carolina, 1975), 41, 50, 60, 74, 91, 187.

16. Perelman and Olbrechts-Tyteca discuss (*The New Rhetoric,* 116–17) the importance of "presence" in argumentation (what the Greeks called *enargeia*): "To create emotion, it is essential to be specific. . . . Whately relates how an audience that had remained unmoved by a general description of the carnage that occurred at the battle of Fontenoy was moved to tears by a little detail concerning the death of two young men" (147). For Demosthenes' use of vivid vignettes, see *On the False Embassy* 64–66, 305–6.

17. Sec. 12.

18. For a discussion of the implications of this term, see Paul Jal, "Hostis (publicus) dans la littérature latine," *Revue des Etudes Anciennes* 41 (1963): 59; and Taddeo, "Signs of Demosthenes," 9.

19. "Hunc igitur ego consulem, hunc civem Romanum, hunc liberum, hunc denique hominem putem?" (12). The climax emphasizes the final term.

20. Cf. *On Oratory* 1.8, 32.

21. Cf. *On Duties* 1.30, 105. This is similar to Cicero's depiction of Catiline and Clodius in earlier speeches (cf. *For Milo* 27 and *Against Catiline* 1.1), and Cicero's use of similar description here only serves to generalize this threat and to connect this attack, the most serious yet, with previous threats to the existence of the state, which Cicero also thwarted.

22. Compare also Cicero's description of Antony's brother, who, like Antony, "fundit apothecas, caedit greges armentorum reliquique pecoris quodcumque nactus est; epulantur milites, ipse autem se, ut fratrem imitetur, obruit vino; vastantur agri, diripiuntur villae, matres familiae, virgines, pueri ingenui abripiuntur, militibus traduntur" (31). In general, Cicero's method of characterization is what one might call "the external approach"; see Robert Scholes and Robert Kellogg, *The Nature of Narrative* (London, 1966), 171−77. Characters are introduced by brief direct narrative statements that describe their attributes, both moral and intellectual. These are then illustrated through their words and deeds, somewhat like the biographies of Suetonius.

23. Taddeo, "Signs of Demosthenes," 12−16.

24. Cf. Cicero, *Philippic III* 31; and Demosthenes, *On the Crown* 66−67.

25. Cf. Liddell and Scott, *Greek-English Lexicon*, 9th ed. rev., s. v. *barbaros*, I; and Demosthenes, *Philippic III* 30−31. In "Signs of Demosthenes," Taddeo says: "Here Cicero illustrates vividly how totally alien in all respects Antony is to the very idea of Romanhood, how indeed he is a second Philip, menacing a second Athens, which a second Demosthenes is determined to defend (11). . . . Both Antony and Philip menaced what the orators believed were the most basic principles of Roman and Athenian constitutional government respectively" (12).

26. For a brief discussion of the use of patterns to reinforce an idea and to hold a speech together, see Wooten, "The Nature of Form," 323−26. Perelman and Olbrechts-Tyteca point out: "The simplest way of creating this presence is by repetition . . . The technique of accumulating, of insisting, is often connected with another technique, that of evoking details" (*The New Rhetoric*, 144−45).

27. Cf. the structure of the *First Philippic* with the proposal beginning at sec. 13; and Blass, *Die Attische Beredsamkeit*, 301−3, 310, 312.

28. Cf. Kennedy, *Art of Persuasion*, 222. See also Marcel Delaunois, "Du plan logique au plan psychologique chez Démosthène," *Les Etudes*

Classiques 19 (1951): 177–89; and "Statistiques des idées dans le cadre du plan oratoire des *Philippiques* de Cicéron," *Les Etudes Classiques* 34 (1966): 3–34.

29. Cf. *On Invention* 1.20–109; and Delaunois, "Du plan logique," 177–89. Also see H. de Raedt, "Plan psychologique de la première *Philippique* de Démosthène," *Les Etudes Classiques* 19 (1951): 227–29; Francis P. Donnelly, "The Argument Used Seventy-two Times in the *Crown Speech* of Demosthenes," *Classical World* 28 (1935): 153–56.

30. Kennedy, *Art of Persuasion*, 229.

31. In "Signs of Demosthenes," Taddeo says: "To this point Cicero has carried the argument to contrasting him with others, such as Octavian, D. Brutus, and Tarquin. Yet as he moves to the second part of the oration, he focuses on Antony directly (16). . . . Previously, the argument was founded on measures which others had taken (Octavian, D. Brutus, the Fourth and Martian legions); now, the proof of the argument is given by Antony himself" (17). This is similar to the approach used in the *Second Philippic*, also Demosthenic, of identifying himself with the audience and gaining their credibility and support before attacking his opponent; cf. Wooten, "Cicero's Reactions," 41–42.

32. Ronnet, *Etude sur le style de Démosthène*," 183–86; Galen Rowe, "Demosthenes' Use of Language," in *Demosthenes' On the Crown*, ed. James Murphy (New York, 1967), 182; Richard C. Jebb, *The Attic Orators from Antiphon to Isaeus*, 2 vols. (London, 1893), 2 : 308–9.

33. Cf. Demosthenes, *Philippic III* 76.

34. Cf. *Philippic I* 2 and *Philippic III* 5.

35. For a general discussion of the appropriateness of such an image in this sort of situation, see Michael Osborn, "Archetypal Metaphor in Rhetoric: The Light-Dark Family," *Quarterly Journal of Speech* 53 (1967): 115–26. As Osborn points out, "Light (and the day) relate to the fundamental struggle for survival" (117); these sorts of images, which reflect clear-cut choices between good and evil and are consequently quite appropriate in these speeches, are found especially "when a society is in upheaval" (126), which is certainly a good description of Roman society during this period.

36. As Demetrius remarks, "To convey much in a few words is more forceful and vehement" (*On Style* 1.7).

37. It is interesting that here (12) Cicero reverses an image that Demosthenes uses in the *First Philippic*. There Philip has cast a net around Athens (10); in Cicero loyal Romans have laid a trap for Antony. The image of Cicero as a soldier (*Philippic IV* 11) is also Demosthenic; cf. *On the Crown* 62.

38. The end of section 13 sounds very similar to Demosthenes' *Philippic III* 36–40 and *On the Crown* 97.

39. George Kennedy, *The Art of Rhetoric in the Roman World* (Princeton, 1972), 278–79; Martin L. Clarke, *Rhetoric at Rome* (London, 1953), 64–65; J. Wight Duff, *A Literary History of Rome*, ed. Arnold M. Duff, 2 vols. (London, 1960), 1:273–74.

40. According to Robin G. M. Nisbet, "The Speeches," in *Cicero*, ed. Thomas A. Dorey (New York, 1965), "Here at least is some of the true Demosthenic 'rapidity' and 'purposefulness'" (76). Cf. also Giovanni Cipriani, *Struttura retorica di dieci orazioni ciceroniane* (Catania, 1975), 340–44. Cicero himself clearly had come to recognize Demosthenes' style as one of the most direct and straightforward ever developed in the ancient world; cf. *Brutus* 35; *Orator* 23, 105, 133, 226, 234; *On the Best Kind of Orators* 17.

41. For a traditional view of Cicero, see Duff, *A Literary History of Rome*, 1:268–69. As George Kennedy points out (*Art of Rhetoric*, 271), this is not necessarily an admirable pose since it hardened the opposition between the senatorial and Caesarian parties.

42. Sec. 2; cf. also sec. 35.

43. My inspiration here, as in much of my work, is an article by Galen Rowe, "Demosthenes' *First Philippic*: The Satiric Mode," *Transactions of the American Philological Association* 99 (1968): 361–74; and I am greatly indebted to him.

44. Ibid., 371–73; the quotation appears on p. 368.

45. Cf. *Philippic I* 47; and Rowe, "Demosthenes' *First Philippic*," 369.

46. Rowe, 363. There are, however, important differences between Demosthenes' use of satire and that of Cicero. In general, Cicero's use of satire is much broader, more extended and sustained, and more obvious than that of Demosthenes. It is also directed more at his opponent than at his audience. Demosthenes' use of satire as a mode of persuasion seems more natural and spontaneous than that of Cicero, who seems, as one would expect of a Roman, to be much more aware of the conventions of a literary genre. On the whole, the basic approach is probably of Demosthenic inspiration; Cicero's techniques, however, doubtless owe much to the conventions of Roman satire.

47. Cf. *Philippic VI*: "Quam, decuit, non tamen omnino dissolute" (1); and "a vobis hanc sententiam repudiari, neque iniuria" (3).

48. The traditional practice in the senate of addressing issues in the order in which they were proposed by the consuls certainly accounts for some of this regularity, although Cicero's treatment is especially patterned.

49. Rowe, "Demosthenes' *First Philippic*," 369.

50. Ibid., 374. For a discussion of what Rowe calls "satire's double vision," see Mary C. Randolph, "The Structural Design of the Formal Verse Satire," *Philological Quarterly* 21 (1942): 372–74.

51. Cf. Galen Rowe, "The Portrait of Aeschines in the Oration *On the Crown*," *Transactions of the American Philological Association* 97 (1966): 397–406.

52. Ibid., 399–402.

53. Ibid., 397–98.

54. Secs. 6–7.

55. There is a problem in the manuscripts between "T. Plancus" and "adolescens nobilis" (10), but it does not extend to this sentence.

56. W. Ross Winterowd, *Contemporary Rhetoric* (New York, 1975), 213.

57. Cf. Robin G. M. Nisbet, ed., *M. Tulli Ciceronis In L. Calpurnium Pisonem Oratio* (Oxford, 1961), 192–97.

Chapter 5

1. Donat Joseph Taddeo, "Signs of Demosthenes in Cicero's *Philippics*" (Ph.D. diss., Stanford University, 1971), 67, comes to the same conclusion. In his discussion of this speech, as in his entire dissertation, which deals only with *Philippics II, III, VII,* and *XIV,* Taddeo is concerned almost exclusively with thematic similarities. Wherever we have reached a similar conclusion, however, I have been careful to refer to his work, which is very good.

2. François de Fénelon, *Lettre à l'Académie,* ed. Ernesta Caldarini (Geneva, 1970), 174; Hugh Blair, *Lectures on Rhetoric and Belles Lettres,* ed. Harold F. Harding, 2 vols. (Carbondale and Edwardsville, 1965), 2 : 12; Lionel Pearson, "The Development of Demosthenes as a Political Orator," *Phoenix* 18 (1964), 96.

3. Pearson, "Development of Demosthenes," 104–5.

4. Ibid., 96.

5. Galen Rowe, "Demosthenes' *First Philippic*: The Satiric Mode," *Transactions of the American Philological Association* 99 (1968): 361.

6. Ibid., 362.

7. Marcel Delaunois, "Statistiques des idées dans le cadre du plan oratoire des *Philippiques* de Cicéron," *Les Etudes Classiques* 34 (1966): 11.

8. Ibid., 27.

9. Pearson, "Development of Demosthenes," 101–2.

10. Ibid., 102.

11. Ibid.

12. Cf. Taddeo, "Signs of Demosthenes," 69–73.

13. Ibid., 71.

14. Alfons Weische, *Ciceros Nachahmung der attischen Redner* (Heidelberg, 1972), 100.

15. Ibid.

16. Werner Jaeger, *Demosthenes: The Origin and Growth of his Policy* (Berkeley, 1938), 42–124.

17. Cf. Taddeo, "Signs of Demosthenes," 93.

18. Joseph Hellegouarch'h, *Le vocabulaire latin des relations et des partis politiques sous la république* (Paris, 1963), 540. Cf. also *Philippic VII*: "Ita, quod erat optabile antea ut populum Romanum comitem haberemus, nunc habemus ducem" (22) which sounds similar to Demosthenes' argument about Olynthus.

19. Werner Jaeger, *Paideia: The Ideals of Greek Culture*, trans. Gilbert Highet, 3 vols. (New York, 1944), 3:263–89.

20. Taddeo, "Signs of Demosthenes," 76.

21. Cf. Cecil Wooten, "The Nature of Form in Demosthenes' *de Corona*," *Classical World* 72 (1979): 325.

22. Cicero uses the same image at the end of the speech: "Etiam summi gubernatores in magnis tempestatibus a vectoribus admoneri solent" (27).

23. Taddeo, "Signs of Demosthenes," 76.

24. This is quite similar, one might argue, to the very regular procedure that Cicero uses in the speech *On the Manilian Law*. There is a great difference, however. Here Cicero is economical, focusing on the most crucial points and developing them as succinctly as possible. There, on the other hand, he is trying to use all the arguments possible; and he also develops them fully, with typically Ciceronian digression and amplification, which makes the argumentation rather diffuse as opposed to the much more direct and rapid argumentation that one finds here. One speech is quite elaborate; the other, relatively simple. The fact that the speech *On the Manilian Law* was delivered at a *contio* before the people and *Philippic VII* was delivered before the senate surely accounts for these differences to a certain extent.

25. Cf. Taddeo, "Signs of Demosthenes," 76–77. Emanuele Castorina, *L'Ultima oratoria di Cicerone* (Catania, 1975), calls this "la *Filippica* più limpide e lineare" (176).

26. George Kennedy, "Focusing of Arguments in Greek Deliberative Oratory," *Transactions of the American Philological Association* 90 (1959): 138.

27. See Cecil Wooten, "Some Observations on Form and Content in Demosthenes," *Phoenix* 31 (1977): 258–61.

28. For an example of Demosthenes' use of a long series of rhetorical questions, see *Olynthiac III* 15–17.

29. Weische points out (*Ciceros Nachahmung*, 158) that Cicero's presentation is generally more vivid and emphatic than that of Demosthenes.

30. Delaunois, "Statistiques des idées," 18.

31. Wooten, "Some Observations," 259.

32. In a very interesting sentence, Cicero makes it clear here that he is using gladiator in its literal sense: "Quem gladiatorem non ita appellavi ut interdum etiam M. Antonius appellari solet, sed ut appellant ei qui plane et Latine loquuntur. Myrmillo in Asia depugnavit" (17).

33. As Taddeo points out ("Signs of Demosthenes," 81), Antony, the new Caesar, attracts all the disreputable characters in the state just as Caesar had done (cf. *Philippic II* 32–78).

34. Cf. Taddeo, "Signs of Demosthenes," 84; and Weische, *Ciceros Nachahmung*, 100, 194.

35. Weische points out (*Ciceros Nachahmung*, 158–62) that one of the differences between Cicero and Demosthenes is Cicero's inclination to develop a thought more briefly than Demosthenes. That inclination is surely evident here.

36. Cf. Taddeo, "Signs of Demosthenes," 85.

37. Cf. Ibid., 88.

38. Chaim Perelman and Lucie Olbrechts-Tyteca, *The New Rhetoric: A Treatise on Argumentation*, trans. John Wilkinson and Purcell Weaver (Notre Dame, 1969), 116–17, 147.

39. Cf. Taddeo, "Signs of Demosthenes," 85.

40. Pearson, "Development of Demosthenes," 104.

41. Taddeo, "Signs of Demosthenes," 89. One might expect the clausulae of this speech to reflect its rapidity and intensity. However, Cicero here mainly uses the double cretic (–‿– | –‿) and cretic plus trochee (–‿– | –‿), which is the case in all the *Philippics* and in Cicero's speeches in general. In this speech, however, unlike the other speeches against Antony, except *Philippics III, XI, XII*, and *XIII*, all of which are quite emotional, he does prefer the double cretic to the cretic plus trochee; and the increased number of light syllables do give the cadences somewhat greater speed. Cf. the chart in Tadeusz Zielinski, *Das Clauselgesetz in Ciceros Reden* (Leipzig, 1904). However, it is really the structure of the sentences as a whole, rather than the clausulae, which gives this speech, and all the *Philippics*, more rapidity. As Louis Laurand says, *Etudes sur le style de Cicéron*, 4th ed., 3 vols. (Paris, 1936–38): "Les clausules sont les mêmes que dans les autres discours. Mais la phrase est plus coupée, moins périodique que dans l'ensemble de l'oeuvre oratoire; le rhythme est plus vif, comme il convient dans une lutte ardente. Quelquefois même, la chute de la phrase a une énergie rude à laquelle Cicéron ne nous avait pas habitués" (3 : 341). Another indication of the directness and simplicity of this speech is the fact that of all the *Philippics* it is the lowest in the average use of participles per page; see Eric Laughton, *The Participle in Cicero* (Oxford, 1964), 140. The *Ninth Philippic*, the most periodic of these speeches, contains the highest average of participles.

Chapter 6

1. For a good discussion of the historical background, general structure, and technical terms in this speech, see Edmond Remy, "La VIIIe *Philippique* de Cicéron," *Les Etudes Classiques* 3 (1934): 458–84 and 7 (1938): 30–40.

2. Galen Rowe, "Demosthenes' Use of Language," in *Demosthenes' On the Crown*, ed. James Murphy (New York, 1967), 196.

3. Ibid.

4. Alfons Weische, *Ciceros Nachahmung der attischen Redner* (Heidelberg, 1972), 158–62.

5. Rowe, "Demosthenes' Use of Language," 182.

6. Ibid., 186. Emanuele Castorina, *L'Ultima oratoria di Cicerone* (Catania, 1975), says: "Appunto la *brevitas* e la *simplicitas dicendi* sono fra le caratteristiche fondamentali di questa oratoria ultima di Cicerone" (155).

7. Rowe, "Demosthenes' Use of Language," 197.

8. Ibid., 187.

9. Ibid., 186.

10. Gilberte Ronnet, *Etude sur le style de Démosthène dans les discours politiques* (Paris, 1951), 163–66.

11. Weische, *Ciceros Nachahmung*, 158–62.

12. Rowe, "Demosthenes' Use of Language," 183–84.

13. Ibid., 362.

14. Ibid., 189–90.

15. L. P. Wilkinson, *Golden Latin Artistry* (Cambridge, 1963), says of this speech: "Rhetoric has been absorbed and disciplined in a style both varied and simple, despite every temptation from the occasion to be fulsome. . . . The style of the *Ninth Philippic* (as compared with the *Pro Archia*) is different and more mature" (182).

16. Lionel Pearson, "The Development of Demosthenes as a Political Orator," *Phoenix* 18 (1964): 105.

17. Ibid., 104.

18. Ibid., 102.

19. Lionel Pearson, *The Art of Demosthenes* (Meisenheim am Glan, 1976), 29.

20. Ibid., 9.

21. Richard McClintock, "Cicero's Narrative Technique in the Judicial Speeches" (Ph.D. diss., University of North Carolina, 1975), 34, 60.

22. Pearson, *The Art of Demosthenes*, 76.

23. Ibid., 73.

24. Ibid., 75.

25. Ibid., 96.

26. McClintock, "Cicero's Narrative Technique," 139.

27. Pearson, *The Art of Demosthenes*, 73.

28. Ibid., 8.

29. Ibid., 81.

30. Ibid., 14–15.

31. Ibid., 44.

32. Ibid., 56.

33. Ibid., 155.

34. Ibid., 56.

35. Ibid., 155.

36. Ibid., 155–56.

37. Ibid., 156; Hermogenes, *On Ideas*, Rabe, 283–84.

38. Pearson, *The Art of Demosthenes*, 192.

39. Ibid., 137.

40. McClintock, "Cicero's Narrative Technique," 39–50.

41. Pearson, *The Art of Demosthenes*, 152.

42. Ibid., 155.

43. For a description of the procedure, see Tsvetan Todorov, *The Poetics of Prose*, trans. Richard Howard (Ithaca, 1977), 151; Ralph Johnson, "Varieties of Narrative in Cicero's Speeches" (Ph.D. diss., University of California, 1967), 145; McClintock, "Cicero's Narrative Technique," 73.

44. Pearson, *The Art of Demosthenes*, vii.

45. Ibid., 78.

46. Johnson, "Varieties of Narrative," 145.

47. Pearson, *The Art of Demosthenes*, 81.

48. Ibid.

49. George Kennedy, "Focusing of Arguments in Greek Deliberative Oratory," *Transactions of the American Philological Association* 90 (1959): 137.

50. One sees in this section, moreover, a difference between Cicero and Demosthenes. Demosthenes uses imagery infrequently and usually explains in detail the comparison that he is making, especially if it is not obvious; cf. Pearson, *The Art of Demosthenes*, 154. Cicero, on the other hand, in many passages, as here, uses images abundantly and does not usually explain them; cf. Weische, *Ciceros Nachahmung*, 158–62. In general, however, the *Philippics* are less imagistic than Cicero's earlier speeches, which may be another Demosthenic influence.

51. Cf. Hermogenes, *On Ideas*, Rabe, 235–37.

52. It is interesting, however, that Cicero is willing to argue against tradition and written law, when it suits his purpose; cf. secs. 27–28 of this speech.

53. It is noteworthy that Cicero also deals with an exception (20), his own proposal to grant an extraordinary command to Octavian. However, an exception to a rule often can be the most convenient way of defining the general rule itself. This is what Cicero does here. Cf. Chaim Perel-

man and Lucie Olbrechts-Tyteca, *The New Rhetoric: A Treatise on Argumentation*, trans. John Wilkinson and Purcell Weaver (Notre Dame, 1969), 356.

54. Cicero's tendency to think in terms of role-models is here emphasized by the fact that he offers himself as a model for Pansa: "Imitare me quem tu semper laudasti: qui instructam ornatamque a senatu provinciam deposui ut incendium patriae omissa omni cogitatione restinguerem" (23).

55. Galen Rowe, "Demosthenes' *First Philippic*: The Satiric Mode," *Transactions of the American Philological Association* 99 (1968): 361.

Chapter 7

1. Lloyd F. Bitzer, "The Rhetorical Situation," *Philosophy and Rhetoric* 1 (1968): 1–14.

2. I am indebted to Professor Robert N. Gaines for showing me his unpublished paper, "Cicero's Rhetorical Situation in the *Philippics*."

3. Bitzer, "The Rhetorical Situation," 6.

4. Hartvig Frisch, *Cicero's Fight for the Republic* (Copenhagen, 1946), 66, 126.

5. Ibid., 137.

6. *Letters to Friends*, 12.3.

7. Frisch, *Cicero's Fight for the Republic*, 143.

8. George Kennedy, *The Art of Rhetoric in the Roman World* (Princeton, 1972), 163.

9. This can be shown statistically, as is demonstrated by a table compiled by Professor Gaines in "Cicero's Rhetorical Situation."

10. Cf. *Letters to Friends* 12.4.

11. That Cicero considered this a personal conflict between himself and Antony is clear from a letter to Brutus, *Letters to Brutus* 1.1.

12. According to the table compiled by Professor Gaines in "Cicero's Rhetorical Situation," the percentage in the first two speeches of Antonian to non-Antonian material is 74 and 66 respectively. In *Philippic XIII*, 58 percent of the speech is devoted to Antony.

13. Donat Joseph Taddeo, "Signs of Demosthenes in Cicero's Philippics" (Ph.D. diss., Stanford University, 1971), 96–119, discusses the Demosthenic influences on this speech, most of which are of the sort already pointed out in detail in earlier chapters in reference to other speeches.

14. Ibid., 96.

15. For a discussion of the panegyric elements in this part of the speech, see Josef Mesk, "Ciceros Nachruf an die legio Martia," *Wiener Studien* 26 (1904): 228–34.

Chapter 8

1. See Cecil Wooten, "Unnoticed Medical Language in Demosthenes," *Hermes* 107 (1979): 159, n. 14. One of the best examples of Cicero's idealization of the past and his search for earlier models is a letter to Atticus (*Letters to Atticus* 8.3) in which he describes the way in which he has tried to make up his mind between Caesar and Pompey during the civil war.

2. For example, Cicero's *Catilinarian Orations* show, as one might expect, many elements of what I have called the "rhetoric of crisis," especially the polarization of good and evil, the contrast between the nobility of the past and the degeneracy of the present, and the tendency to assume role-models. Cicero, however, sees the threat from Catiline more in terms of other threats to the republican constitution during the end of the second and the first half of the first century (cf. *Against Catiline* 1.4); and the argument that the very existence of the state is in danger seems more a rhetorical ploy than in the *Philippics*, where it is taken very seriously. Also, there is no recognizable influence of Demosthenes on these speeches, which also makes them different from the *Philippics*.

3. Winston Churchill, "Prime Minister," in *Blood, Sweat, and Tears*, ed. Randolph Churchill (New York, 1941), 276.

4. Ibid.

5. Ibid.

6. Ibid.

7. Cf. Michael Osborn, "Archetypal Metaphor in Rhetoric: The Light-Dark Family," *Quarterly Journal of Speech* 53 (1967): 119–20.

8. Winston Churchill, "Their Finest Hour," in *Blood, Sweat, and Tears*, ed. Randolph Churchill, 314.

9. Winston Churchill, "Every Man to His Post," in ibid., 369.

10. I am grateful to an anonymous reader of this manuscript for calling my attention to the possible implication that Philip and Antony were in the same category as Hitler, which I certainly do not mean to imply, in spite of the depiction that one finds in Cicero and Demosthenes. World War II was much more clearly black and white than were the conflicts in which Demosthenes and Cicero were involved, although it may have been less black and white than Churchill made it seem. Moreover, I do not mean to imply that self-interest and nobility, especially in men of heroic stature, are incompatible. Often the most noble of deeds are performed for the most selfish of reasons.

11. Osborn, "Archetypal Metaphor in Rhetoric," 120.

12. Winston Churchill, "To the French People," in *Blood, Sweat, and Tears*, ed. Randolph Churchill, 403.

Index